# A
# WARTIME
# Christmas

# A WARTIME Christmas

*Compiled by*
MARIA & ANDREW HUBERT

SUTTON PUBLISHING

First published in the United Kingdom in 1995 by
Sutton Publishing Limited
Phoenix Mill · Thrupp · Stroud · Gloucestershire GL5 2BU

Reprinted 1996, 1997, 1999, 2000, 2002

British Library Cataloguing in Publication Data
A catalogue record for this book is avialble from the British Library

Typeset in Garamond 12/13.
Typesetting and origination by
Sutton Publishing Limited.
Printed in Great Britain by
J.H. Haynes & Co. Ltd, Sparkford.

# Dedication

We have tried to gather a goodly selection of happy and sad, funny and serious stories, and from as many different backgrounds as possible. The chronological accounts have been interspersed with lighter chapters, looking at aspects on the Kitchen Front, the Home Front, ENSA, and even a ghost story. Sadly, there are a great number of unsung heroes and heroines who have not had their stories told in this volume, and for all the regiments, squadrons, ships' companies and the civilian groups we have mentioned here, there are so very many more not included. To them, as to those included, and to all war veterans everywhere – we offer this book of wartime Christmas as a tribute to your courage, endurance, humour and faith.

# Contents

# A Wartime Christmas

# Spend At Christmas!

## EDWARD HULTON

*In* Picture Post *(9 December 1939), the editor, Edward Hulton,
exhorted people to spend, and then spend some more, for the war effort.
As we are usually a little guilty about all the money we spend at
Christmas, this must have provided people with the perfect excuse to do just
that. One wonders, however, just how many ordinary folk had money
spare that Christmas!*

It is our duty to spend – either on Savings Certificates or ordinary
goods. There must be no idle 'talents'. And a long face never won a war.

What shall we do about Christmas? This is the season when we are
usually thinking about making those purchases, which may be
somewhat pointless, are often a vexation of spirit, but are nevertheless a
great stimulus to trade. In the present circumstances many people are
asking, ought we celebrate Christmas at all? There can be no doubt
that this is the very year when we should think, not less, but more
about Christmas – not only as an escape from the horrors of war, but as
a remembrance of nobler ideals. . . . In being cheerful and gay we are
paying our tribute to life itself, which must go on, and which, after all,
is what man is fighting for. . . . Let us hope that women will make the
season an excuse to be somewhat more decorative.

Nowhere do we show a greater lack of proportion than in our
spending habits. For the very poor there is no dilemma. But in normal
times most of us have some surplus. Spending wisely is the one thing
our parents never teach us. The whole subject of money is more taboo
than sex. . . . Let us seize this season to think again. We may spend on
the new National Savings Certificates (and War Bonds), or on ordinary
purchases. But no money must be left idle.

And if we are merry at Christmas, we shall be showing the Nazis
that we are winning the war of nerves, and maintaining the gallant
spirit which has overcome the adversities which are no novelty to the
very windswept isle.

Official advertisement for War Bonds and National Savings Certificates – even as Christmas presents these released money for the war effort in return for a guaranteed profit. Good in the 1940s; not so good for those who hung on into the 1980s! (Christmas Archives)

*from*

# They Tied a Label on my Coat

## HILDA HOLLINGSWORTH

*Miss Hollingsworth's account of her own evacuation during the Second World War tells of four very different Christmases. Propaganda always described those children who had found homes better than their own, happy times filled with sunshine and haymaking and full creamy milk, and snow and presents better than anything Mum could afford. But much of the reality went unrecorded, except in books such as this one. Here is an extract of Hilda's first Christmas — the only really happy one — where the two sisters awake to find that, although Mum may not have come, Santa had.*

''Ild, 'Ild, Wake up! 'E's bin! Santa's *bin*! Come an' feel . . .'

Auntie had said we could switch on the light. Our woolly stockings bulged temptingly. Sticking out of the top of each was a celluloid doll with feathers stuck around waist and head. I delved inside. A rolled sheet of transfers. Picture colouring book. Paints, with names like Vermillion, Indigo and Yellow Ochre. A round wooden pillbox full of hundreds and thousands. A whip and top. Chocolate medal. A bright new penny. Then the apple and orange that today were just usual, and right deep inside the toe the three nuts which Mum always called Faith, 'Ope and Charity. I never knew why.

I picked up the metal canister. It was disappointing. There was nothing inside it. I turned it upside down. 'Gas Mask Container' said the label. I laid it beside the woolly stocking. The real treasure was the *other* one: the coarse white net stocking edged with frilly crêpe paper. Its wonders had delighted us year after year. Rolled cardboard games of Ludo and Snakes-and-Ladders. A kazoo. A feathered streamer that

Evacuee children making the best of the situation at a London council party.
(Christmas Archives)

squeaked and tickled. A cardboard trumpet and a tin frog clicker. A tin whistle. A big coloured picture of Father Christmas. A game of five-stones that we never played because it hurt our hands. A net-covered silver paper ball on thin elastic; I really liked that. Tiny tin scales with two miniature sweet jars full of tiny sweets to weigh on them. A box of coloured chalks. Another delight: Japanese water flowers. I think these were always my favourite because I never did get over the wonder of the little round wood shavings that opened and bloomed instantly in a glass of water.

The fat little flicker book. I flicked the pages and saw matchstick men running, jumping, swinging whilst matchstick ladies pushed

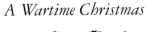

prams, danced and skipped. It was marvellous: a sort of moving story that you could only see, never hear. Next came a paper fan and then a peashooter, the dried peas in a twist of paper. Mum had always taken this delight away; I wondered if Auntie would.

We were near the end now. A card of coloured Plasticine, and – deep in the toe – a little sorbo ball. It was the same every year. Nothing ever changed. We didn't know it ever would. So we now sat facing one another wondering what to do next. The transfers. We each made a careful wet-spit patch on our forearm and applied the picture – mine was a galleon, Pat's a stagecoach – face down. Then with much licking, we managed to wet it into position. Now we had to count to fifty. Pat waited to see me peel back the first corner. I held my breath, peeling slowly . . . watching the bright damp shiny colours miraculously choosing to stay on my waiting arm . . . Yippee! I'd got the whole picture first time! . . .

Roast pork and plum pudding; Auntie's house was full of lovely smells – smells of a new part of Christmas that Auntie knew about. Our own Christmas smell was . . . well, I hadn't really realized we had one just like Auntie's, till I was helping arrange her bowl of nuts and fruit and crystallized figs. A smell from the fruit bowl has a Christmas smell . . . Oranges! Soon all three of us were sniffing at them. Auntie laughed. 'Oh *have* one! But don't spoil your dinners.' That's what was worrying me too. And I don't suppose Auntie ever knew that we *really* peeled our oranges just to get the smell.

# Saturday Night Conscription

## NORMAN BISHOP

*Norman Bishop, now in his seventies, amuses his customers with stories of how he used to '. . . travel in ladies' underwear', or how he met his wife in the blackout, so she didn't know what she was getting. His war was spent with anti-aircraft batteries in South Wales.*

I went off to war by accident. As a Territorial Army volunteer, I took leave from my office for a fortnight's camp at Manorbier in South Wales. While I was away, war was declared, and I was now operational, so my fortnight's leave from the office lasted for six years!

When I began active service, the equipment and clothing was very substandard. Being with the artillery, I found myself wearing 1914–18 vintage spurs and puttees! We had no proper facilities at all; we all camped under canvas, shaving in the open air. Not much fun in Newport with winter looming!

Christmases were such that the 'Militia Men' (as such conscriptees were known until 1941), would have taken any form of Christmas celebration, as long as it was alcoholic. Once the real war got under way, it was very important to keep morale up, and efforts were made to entertain the anti-aircraft gun crews.

The major problem was one of boredom. Although I was ultimately responsible for gun emplacements around Barry, Cardiff and Newport, which meant that on many nights there was 'traffic' for us, particularly with bombers overflying from France via Wales to the Mersey, individual gun emplacements could be on stand-by for many hours in the damp and cold, without any action.

Our HQ and ops room had a couple of local moves, eventually fetching up at a requisitioned large house – Penylan Court in Cardiff.

The HQ coordinated the anti-aircraft fire from 3.7 in and 4.5 in guns which were mounted by twos, together with a complicated sighting device known as a predictor, in emplacements which could be moved around in order to confuse enemy planners.

By 1943, my job comprised standing behind a glass screen, plotting aircraft movements which were reported by RDF (radio direction finding, later called radar), and writing any relevant information such as height and size in mirror writing – a skill that was quickly learned.

Vital though my job undoubtedly was, I was not promoted above bombardier, as it was thought that the relative comfort of HQ with its heating, and ATS girls, were compensation enough, for the former rigours of life under canvas. I was encouraged, however, to tinkle the old ivories, in order to assist the general war effort, and there was no objection to swapping duties with others in order to cover special events.

Christmas was one of those special events. There was unfortunately one minor hitch. We had made up a combo using the available talent, but we had no saxophonist. In those days, a saxophonist was vital for any dance band worthy of the name, and Christmas without a dance, wasn't worth celebrating.

This problem was circumvented by the addition of a 'civvie' saxophonist, who found himself temporarily conscripted on Saturday nights, high days and holidays.

So for a number of years, my service Christmas consisted of wangling exchanges for various duties, having Christmas dinner served by the officers (an old army tradition), and laying on some sort of music for a dance in the evening, complete with willing civilian. As for decorations, there were few. The important thing was to get the music going, keep the drinking and conversation good natured, and allow everyone to let their hair down, because tomorrow the war would still be waiting for them.

*from*

# Dear Merv – Dear Bill: 1

## MERVYN HAISMAN AND L.E. SNELLGROVE

*Two schoolboy friends from south-east London, torn apart by the mass
evacuations in 1939, created a valuable social document in their
three-year correspondence. Here we reproduce their Christmas letters.*

**3 December 1939** – . . . We've been away three months now and I'm
beginning to really miss Mum and Dad. Of course I can't tell them
that, as it would only upset them. I expect you'll be having one of your
big family Christmas parties as usual. They say we should have plenty
of snow down here, so at least that's something to look forward to.
Write soon. Your friend, Merv.

**2 January 1940** – Dear Merv, Happy New Year old bean! I told
Roberts that it was so long since I'd last seen you, I'd begun to forget
what you looked like. He reckoned I was very, very lucky!

Did you have a good Christmas? I must say I felt sorry for you for
the first time since the war began, not being at home and all that. Just
before Christmas I popped around to Kenward Road to give your mum
and dad a Christmas card. I think they are missing you too, although
they don't actually say so. They said you didn't write very often. I
hadn't the heart to tell them you were too busy sending me war
communiqués. Which reminds me, thanks for the warning about
Alma. I think her backside is better now, she certainly wiggles it a lot!

It's freezing cold here, but we had a good family Christmas at my
Aunt Ada's house in Plumstead. All my strange uncles and aunts were
there with their children, John, Ken, Ron and Brenda who are great
fun. Cousin John was evacuated to Ashford in Kent but he's back now
and will be going to my school. We heard the King's broadcast about
talking to the man at the gate of the year, which went down well.
They've got copies of it stuck up in Montagu Burton's window in the
High Street.

My grandfather who fought in the Boer War, and Dad who fought in the First World War, get a lot of amusement from the war bulletins on the radio, because the only raids we seem to carry out are not to drop bombs but leaflets telling the Germans to give up. I ask you! This is the army that took us four years to beat last time. Grandad's favourite bulletin is, 'A lorry was seen to overturn'. He says they could have done that in the Boer War before aeroplanes were invented.

We played Aunt Ada's favourite game, Nuts in May, which has a lot of tugging in it and as John and Ken are as big as me, was a lot of fun. All my uncles sat for hours and hours playing cards, then spent just as long arguing over who laid the wrong trump and all that sort of rot. But on Christmas morning I was allowed to go round to the Nag's Head with the men. Just as we'd started to really enjoy ourselves, Aunt Ada marched in and said dinner was waiting. When I'm grown up no woman's going to drag me out of a pub.

Dad reckons this 'phoney war' as they call it, won't last much longer and says that when it really does start, it'll be worse than last time and take six years not four. He says that all we seem to have at the moment is an army of crooners singing, 'We're going to hang out the washing on the Siegfried line'. Two of my uncles are young enough to be called up. I wonder if they'll be with us next Christmas?

Back home, I went on writing my life of Napoleon. I'm up to the Battle of Wagram in 1809, so there's still a lot to do. The exercise book situation is terrible. At school we've only been using sheets of paper. If I tried to smuggle any of it out of school, Haggar would enjoy skinning me alive because he's already taken a dislike to me. He says I'm big-headed. I know I am but unlike him I've got something to be big-headed about. After all, where's his life of Napoleon? Cheerio, write soon, Bill.

# Polish Carols – Symbol of Yearning for Home

## JAN SLIWINSKI

*In December 1940 Jan Sliwinski published a book of Polish Christmas carols, the proceeds going to the Polish Red Cross. Polish carols are uniquely different. They have tunes which can be as simple as a nursery rhyme or as complex as a great and glorious oratorio. The task of the carol is, according to an old Polish manuscript, to 'amuse and lull the Christchild to sleep'. In his dedication Jan Sliwinski remembers the soldiers with tears in their eyes, singing these carols from their very souls all through the long years of the Second World War, as they did when he was in Poland in 1915.*

December in Poland can be sometimes very cold. The snow will crunch under your steps, the biting frost will make the firs and pines crack in their branches and the breath of men and animals will steam like boiling water.

I remember such a December in 1915 when we Polish legionaries in the Volhynian forests were standing under the starry sky for the midnight mass. The soldiers' voices singing carols filled the air with a heavenly warmth and sweetness.

Wherever a Polish carol will be sung, there will be warmth and sweetness. . . .

. . . These traditional Polish carols are meant to turn the blood of war into the balm of love. British children will sing them for their starving Polish brothers and sisters. May they always be performed for the benefit of children.

For six long war winters the Polish soldier has sung these carols in many foreign lands and found comfort in them. The Polish carol has become the unacknowledged symbol of the exile's yearning for home.

# Merrily to Bethlehem

*A seventeenth-century folktune arranged by Kaźimierz Hubert von Staufer.*

# Memories of a Survivor

## TOMASZ HUBERT

*Tomasz Hubert is one of life's survivors. He has survived Siberia, starvation, typhus, plane crashes, flak, dogfights, car crashes, motorcycle crashes, fractured skulls (note the plural), meningitis and a stroke. Apart from gout and angina, he leads a normal life (if indeed his life has ever been normal).*

Polish Christmases are always a serious matter of tradition. Preparations in a Polish household before the war always went on for weeks. The Polish *materfamilias* had a great amount of baking, pickling, salting and provisioning to do. There always would have been help from servants and daughters to make sure that everything from the *barszcz* (a festive beetroot soup) to the *makowiec* (poppyseed roll) were ready for Christmas Eve. Freshwater fish, particularly carp, formed the basis of *Wigilia* (the Christmas Eve celebration). Usually such fish were bought alive, as refrigeration had not really arrived in south-eastern Poland. That is how one of my elder sisters came to object upon finding a live pike in the bath!

After my father had died, my mother found it difficult providing everything, especially as I was the only man in the family, and I was a student. A great deal of effort had been made for that final Christmas before the war, and although it was a scene of frantic activity and some worry, it turned out to be a very good humoured affair. None of us had any idea that it would be the last Christmas we would celebrate together.

I was gliding when the order for general mobilization came through on the last day of August 1939. The next day, the war was fully under way by mid-morning. In Lwów we didn't see very much action, until the Russians took a hand.

As I was a boy scout, I attached myself to a field hospital, which was a very shocking experience for someone approaching his eighteenth birthday. Once all resistance had been crushed, we were all ordered to report to our colleges or places of work, then they arrested us. My father had been a colonel with Marshal Pilsudski, in the fight against the Bolsheviks in 1919–21. I think that made me a marked man, a political prisoner.

That Christmas of 1939 found me in a one-man cell jammed in with so many others that lying down was impossible. We all sang carols to raise our spirits as there was no heating: it was bitterly cold. We were allowed a minuscule sugar ration for nourishment. A doctor who was imprisoned with us was very anxious that we should not do without our ration, as it was the only thing keeping us alive.

Some inmates traded their sugar for tobacco, which was signing their own death warrant in more ways than one. The Russians had allowed one Christmas parcel consisting of about a kilo or more of tobacco but only five packets of cigarette papers! Hunger gnawed at us, and having nothing else to do I took up smoking. The doctor didn't think that was such a good idea either, but I did keep my sugar ration, and did not tempt anyone else into giving up theirs, by trading my tobacco or cigarette papers. So my Christmas present to myself for 1939 was the habit of smoking.

If I had thought that 1939 was bad, Vorkuta (a miserable unsafe slave mining camp in the Northern Urals) ensured that Christmas 1940 was even worse. I was among only four Poles, totally outnumbered by hundreds of Russian political prisoners, all victims of Stalin's policies. We were hated by many of the Russian inmates as well as the Bolshevik guards, so Christmas was observed in silent recollection if we got the chance at all.

By the end of 1941, we had escaped into the Siberian winter. The Russian criminals who had forced an exit while the guards were drunk, seemed to have taken us Poles along either as beasts of burden, or to supplement their protein intake. We were not going to wait to find out. We joined a working party from another prison camp, and were smuggled into their hard labour camp! That is where we learned of the amnesty for Poles since the German attack on Russia.

Christmas was lost in a battle for survival, as we worked our way southwards armed with forged release documents, joining ever more Poles as we foraged on our way through Russia, Kazakhstan and

Tomasz Hubert on the journey south through Iran in 1941; note the rags wrapped around the worn-out boots and the ragged coat. (Angela and Tomasz Hubert)

Uzbekistan, to the major rallying points for Polish soldiers in Palestine and Iran. Clothing was at a premium, I only had rags and a quilted *kufaika* for protection against temperatures of minus fifty or so.

My next Christmas was a great improvement. By 1942, I was a pilot under training for the RAF in England. Christmas trees, quite reasonable food (if not all the elements of the Polish Christmas Eve) and Midnight Mass were a reality. Many Poles used considerable ingenuity to secure those little luxuries which meant such a lot. Many of us had acquired English girlfriends, so attempts were made to wangle any leave for home visits over the Christmas period.

I was not flying operationally by Christmas 1943, but I had become engaged to an English girl who lived just outside Brighton, so I succeeded in getting some time off to be entertained by her mother and sisters, who had an open house at Christmas time. The festivities were a blend of whatever could be scrounged and put together. Not really Polish, but not really English either.

Autumn 1944 was a period of intense flying and exhaustion as our Spitfires attacked anything that moved across the roads of Belgium, Holland and Germany. We were frequently on the move, taking over hurriedly cleared fields in mud and later snow, or occupying deserted ex-Luftwaffe airfields. The Germans had begun the Ardennes offensive by Christmas of that year, but I still managed to find some aircraft delivery excuse to bring me back for a few hours with the English girl who was now my wife. The stress of wartime flying was such, and so many friends had been killed, that the overwhelming Christmas memory is one of relaxation and no war for a few hours!

New Year's Day 1945 was for me a very cold and snowy early start on an armed reconnaissance mission. By the time we returned, we had used up most of our Spitfires' fuel.

We were surprised to find our home field under attack. Flames from burning aircraft and fuel dumps were billowing into the air, as German aircraft criss-crossed the field. Their Focke Wulfs were of the latest type, very fast, and very difficult to catch. I had some success, but one of my squadron was credited with downing two, without firing his guns! He ran out of fuel and landed on a road, making two Focke Wulfs that had appeared beneath him split right and left, crashing on either side of the road!

Although we had many more months of intense flak to endure, and were to lose so many friends, this was the last major effort by the Luftwaffe, and the violent end of my last wartime Christmas season.

# Wot No Christmas Spirit?

RON WILLIAMS

*The cartoon figure of Mr Chad poking his nose over a brick wall,
protesting about wartime shortages with the inevitable caption: 'Wot no
bananas' (sugar, cheese, beef, etc.) came to symbolize how much
circumstances had changed. From the following story it would appear that
rationing had extended to the milk of human kindness long before any
other wartime exigencies had made their impact.
Ron Williams today is a very active pensioner living in Herefordshire.
Perhaps his need to address injustice was born in the cold grey light of
that first wartime Christmas morning.*

I was called up at the outbreak of war and found myself posted to the
Royal Artillery. By Christmas 1939 I had been sent to serve at
Harwich, where the routine was one of endless guard duty and
unrelieved boredom.

By and large, any National Service conscriptee or volunteer was
regarded with acute suspicion and disdain by the regular soldiers of all
ranks. The NCOs particularly insisted that every task be performed 'by
the book', regardless of its stupidity during the wartime emergency.
Morale among the men was of little interest to them; discipline and
mindless routine were the things that made them tick, and they
expected no less from us servicemen notwithstanding our backgrounds,
strengths, weaknesses, or other qualities. The idea of capitalizing on
other experience in order to get the job done was an alien concept.

I had been on sentry duty until very late on Christmas Eve, and had
shaved before turning in, hopeful of saving a few minutes when I had
to get up for sentry duty at the crack of dawn (05.00 hours).

I was tired and cold, it was not very Christmassy, and the tedium of

''Ave you shaved this morning?' – wartime-style cartoon by Giles Thomas.
(Copyright Giles Thomas, 1995)

standing guard outside in the dank air weighed very heavily on me.

As the morning progressed, an officer accompanied by the sergeant-major (very much the regular soldier, no time for us National Service types), came round to wish all the various guards a Happy Christmas. When the officer got to me, he duly wished me the compliments of the season and passed on. The sergeant-major, however, had other ideas. He paused as the officer walked away.

'Gunner Williams, have you shaved this morning?'

'No Sergeant-Major, I shaved last night.'

'You're on a charge!'

Where's the Christmas spirit? I asked myself; it was obviously an early casualty of the war.

I had the last laugh in a manner of speaking, as later that day I came down with a bad dose of food poisoning. (So much for Army Christmas dinners. The catering corps had a lot to answer for.) I spent the next few weeks in hospital, then was immediately posted away, as the war situation was becoming ugly.

I suppose that the only present the Royal Artillery gave me that year, was not having to answer the charge! I was not really very impressed by my introduction to Christmases spent in wartime service.

# Christmas Message – 1939

## ARCHBISHOP OF YORK

*In his pastoral address for Christmas 1939, the Archbishop of York attempted to capture the mood of the time, directing the thoughts of his flock towards the prospect of a kinder world, what Churchill a few months later would describe as the 'broad sunlit uplands'.*

The call of Christmas sounds strangely in time of war – but far more strangely to those who have forgotten the origin of the festival. We have so often let it become a feast of innocence (but the Bible knows nothing of human innocence), or a festival of childhood (but the Bible nowhere suggests that childhood is exempt from danger). The Christian faith has no illusions about the sort of world into which Christ was born and in which his message has to be proclaimed.

> Yet with the woes of sin and strife
> The World has suffered long;
> Beneath the Angel strain have rolled
> Two thousand years of wrong;
> And man at war with man, hears not
> The love song which they bring:
> O hush the noise, ye men of strife
> And hear the Angel sing.

'The World was made by Him, and the World knew Him not. He came to His own home and His own people received Him not.' That is part of the authentic Christmas message. We are relieved from some shock and disappointment if we remember this.

Christmas as a purely secular festival has a charm of its own; and in a world so full of ugliness and misery one is grateful for every element of joy or charm. But if that is all that can be said, it is no more than an oasis in the world's desert, or (worse still) a means of escape from grim reality into a realm of delightful fantasy. Such an escape is almost always bad for us; ask the psychologists! What we want is not escape from reality but courage to transform it. Christmas can give us both of these in abundance.

Childhood is not all joy; the tears of childhood are frequent and very bitter. The eternal God shares the weakness of childhood; this is the marvel, 'That He, the olde Eternal Worde, should be a Childe and weepe.'

Into our simplest and deepest sorrow God has entered: as we bear it, He is with us, not with the detached benevolence sometimes mis-called sympathy, but with the 'fellow feeling' which the word 'sympathy' truly means. Fellowship with God is the greatest of all sources of endurance.

But it is not enough to endure bravely the horrors of the world with its strifes and wars. We want to transform the world and end its wars. If that is to happen there must grow up in us a spirit of real goodwill strong enough to resist the influences which divide men from each other – man from man, class from class, nation from nation, race from race. It is no manner of use to try to generate that spirit by making up our minds to it. Any of us who are honest with ourselves know quite well that amiable sentiments, which are all that we can conjure up in ourselves, are powerless against either strong financial interests or nationalist passions. That is why 'uplift' cuts no morsel of this frosty world's ice!

But if we find out what worship is, and then try actually to worship the Divine Child for whom there was 'no room at the inn', it begins to work in us the transformation which enables us to set about the transformation of the world and is, in fact, the beginning of it. For pride and exclusiveness and envy and contempt are all alike obliterated by that worship. And in it we are all united. On Christmas morning German Christians, French Christians, Polish Christians, Finnish

Christians, British Christians, Russian Christians – let us never forget the heroic multitude of Russian Christians – nor the Japanese and Chinese who in the name of Christ are all this time making unity which will unite their nations as friends in days to come – all these in the depth of their being are crowding round the Child who lies in the feeding trough of kindly beasts, and on whom their hopes for this world as truly as for the next are set.

> Our God, heaven cannot hold Him
> Nor earth sustain;
> Heaven and earth shall flee away
> When he comes to reign.
> In the bleak mid-winter
> A stable place sufficed
> The Lord God Almighty
> Jesus Christ.

Christmas is the season of peace and goodwill; but it is something else first – the season for giving glory to God in the highest. When mankind is ready to do that, it will find the peace and goodwill which it knows to be its greatest need.

# A Strange Christmas – 1939

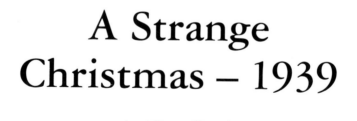

*The first Christmas of the war was the first Christmas this century when Britain saw massive social upheaval as a result of civilians being affected by war. To most Britons any foreigner was an unfamiliar sight, but by 1945 British insularity had gone forever. Here are some contemporary*

# A Wartime Christmas

*news reports about the impact of a British Christmas on refugees, and British families affected by the war, as reported in the* Picture Post *for Christmas 1939.*

This is the story of six lots of children whose Christmas has been made different by the war. Different from what it would have been if Hitler had not invaded Poland. Different from what it would have been if the father of one of them had not lost his job through the war. Or if the father of another had not been shot down by German aircraft over the Western Front. Or if the mother of another had not walked up the gangway of a ship which was soon to strike a mine and go down with her and many others. A look at contemporary news reports from Christmas periodicals, 1939.

The war affected everybody's children. But not all children notice the war all the time. For many it is often only a pleasant disturbance of the familiar routine. But to disturb the routine of Christmas – to break up the family then – is another thing. It is at Christmas when they think back to 'what we were all doing this time last year' that they know something quite out of the ordinary must be happening in the outside world. They realize that they too, are in this war.

There are the four Dutch children saved from the *Simon Bolivar* when it struck a mine and sank off the East Coast on 18 November. No one knew the name of one of these children, a little chap of about nine months old, so they called him Simon after the ship, until someone could come along who could put his proper name to him. The other children's parents soon came to claim them, one even remembered talking to Simon's mother on the ship, a surname like 'Renier'. But no one has come forward for him. He is suffering from bronchitis and shock but is much better than he was.

Yolanda is a Polish refugee living now in Britain. Her family was well-to-do, and lived in Gdynia. When shells fell on her home town, her mother told her to take her brother Stefan and flee to Lithuania. It took them three months to reach Britain. They have no money left; Stefan goes to a London school in his one suit. Yolanda has but one frock apart from her school uniform. They do not like their surname known in case it rebounds on their father and friends back in Nazi-occupied Poland. Their father fought in the Polish Army and was taken prisoner outside Danzig; he has not been heard of since. Now the brother and sister are being sent to Catholic schools, but they will not see each other at Christmas; they have nowhere to meet.

Young Gladys Hanks is one of Britain's many evacuee children. One of the tens of thousands who were uprooted from all they held secure, and sent to safer places away from the bombs – and their families. She will spend Christmas in Cambridge, some fifty miles away from home. There are lots of interesting things to do, such as exploring the cattle market for instance.

Orphans of the lost *Courageous*, these two sets of twins, Alan, Peter, Bobby and David Jones are only aged six and three. Luckily they were too young to feel the full shock of the news of the loss of *Courageous*, the torpedoed aircraft carrier on which their father was a stoker. They now live in Dr Barnardo's home near Plymouth and their life is so full and interesting that they have as yet little time to remember. After breakfast on Christmas Day there will be stockings and later carols. There will be a Christmas tree in the window, and Mr Cobbold the superintendent will dress up as Father Christmas.

Two sets of twins orphaned by the war. (Christmas Archives)

John Robert Gravely's father is a hero, though John is too young to understand just yet. He pulled his wounded air observer from their shot-down aircraft, and despite being badly burned himself, returned for the air gunner, who was unfortunately already dead. He will receive the OBE for this gallantry. All that concerns John junior is whether his father will be home for Christmas.

John Warrington has eleven children; two married, the rest at home – and he has lost his job. An old soldier, he joined the Army again at the outbreak of war, at the age of 49, with a weak chest; after a couple of months he was discharged because of it. So with Christmas in sight he is without a job. The children are gay and healthy and their mother struggles to keep them decently dressed; when the war came and took her husband's job away, it lessened her housekeeping, but not their growing appetites, which they will still have at Christmas, whether their father gets another job or no.

There is one group of young evacuees who will enjoy their Christmas this year. They are the children from the Hutton residential school at Shenfield in Essex. This party was partly sponsored by a London magazine, but throughout the country, evacuated London children were able to enjoy parties because of a fund set up by the London County Council for just that purpose, so that Hitler or no Hitler, the youngsters will not be deprived of the greatest treat of the year.

These are the tales of just a few of the children whose lives have been changed by the war, whose futures will no longer be the same as they would have been, whose Christmases will not be merry.

# The Ghost of El Ageila

## F.G.H. SALUSBURY

*One does not necessarily associate wartime with ghost stories, yet the Second World War was to provide many, ranging from phantom pilots to ghost ships. Perhaps the stress of mechanized war made the human psyche more responsive to paranormal stimuli. Here is an account, published under a* nom de plume *for security reasons, that was printed in the* Daily Express *just before Christmas 1942. No amount of research has been able to discover any identity for the author of this piece, but it is believed to have been an authentic account from a serving officer.*

Dusk was coming down like a cold, wet blanket over Ageila and the venomous thickly-mined trail of the enemy.

To the north the Mediterranean grumbled coldly at the salt marshes; to the south, the bad country was approached with chilly diffidence by flat stretches of mud and desolation.

The sergeant of the sappers, sitting under the lee of a truck drawn up close to the roadside, swilled his tea round and round the mug to collect the last sediment of sugar, and wished he had a toothpick.

'It's wonderful', he said, 'how bully clings to the teeth. The slightest foothold – blimey, it's wonderful. Nothing short of blasting . . .'

The man at his elbow interrupted him with a grunt of pure amazement. He said, 'My God! Look at that!'

It is curious how strong language of the traditional kind sometimes fails in really tense moments.

'Oh dear', murmured the sergeant, following his neighbour's gaze. He swallowed the last of his tea, put his mug on the ground and got slowly to his feet.

'The blue-nosed basket!' breathed another man. 'He's got a chance in a thousand.'

'Two thousand', said the sergeant, 'more like.'

They were all watching a truck which was perhaps half a mile away

and approaching them at a good pace. There was nothing unusual in that – one of the commonest sights of the desert – but the coldness about them took on a sharper edge, and their muscles contracted because of their specialized knowledge. They knew, none better, that the only negotiable strip of ground in that neighbourhood lay along the road which it had been their devoted task to clear of mines.

The truck they were watching was well out into the waste, where mines were as thick as peas. Whence it came and how it got there – they were not worried about that.

They wondered only how long the driver would survive. The sergeant said suddenly, 'He's drunk.' And the truck certainly moved as if under some sort of inspired control. It zig-zagged joyously, darting to the south, hiccuping, stopping, starting again and darting off again to the north. But always with the sergeant's place by the road as its guiding objective.

'Wait for it', whispered the man who had first noticed the truck, as if in quiet enjoyment of a conjuring trick, and the sergeant ran out into the desert bellowing a warning.

The truck stopped for a couple of minutes and then, 'My God, he's off again!' – it seemed to pull itself together and with all the genius of the drunk for safely crossing a place like Piccadilly Circus in a pre-war rush hour, made straight for the sergeant and pulled up twenty feet away.

A head appeared out of the driver's cabin, and a tired cockney voice asked, 'Orright for the road mates?'

'All right for ruddy death', exploded the sergeant. 'What the hell do you think you've been doing – driving all over the burning desert and those incarnadine mines like a flaming camel?'

The driver dropped out of his cabin and stood flapping wearily with one hand as if to ward off the shower of words.

'Don't arsk me Sarge,' he cut in, 'you arsk the orfficer.'

'Officer?' repeated the sergeant.

'I got a bit off the road I admit,' said the driver, 'some way back, an' I see where a bloke has just gorn an copped one just in front of me see. And I'm just wonderin' what to do when the orfficer comes up and says, "Go on," he says, "I know the way through this little lot," he says, "I been here before," he says see.

'So what could I do but say, "Yessir." So in he gets and orf we go and he says to me very sharp, "When I say right you go right, and when I say left you go left, and don't you hesitate," he says. "I know what I'm

about and no ruddy error, I been here before," he says.'

'You acted as if you'd gone crazy', said one of the sappers. 'Or were right. Left right, left right, strewth!'

'I know,' said the driver. 'That's when the orfficer tells me to stop and then – after I hears you hollering Sarge – he says to me, "Here, this is where I get off," he says. "Make straight for those sappers," he says, "and don't you go a ruddy step further without them telling you. This is as far as I go," he says, "but you'll be orlright now see."'

'The officer got out of your truck when you pulled up?' said the sergeant.

'That's right, you see him didn't you, when I pulled up just after you hollered. An' the funny thing was, I says to him as he got out, "You got a nerve sir," I says, "going through all these mines like that." And he says, "I got no nerves now." He says, "Those are things you leave behind." And then he hops out and I come on see.'

There was an uncomfortable pause. A sapper cleared his throat. The sergeant said, very slowly, 'No officer got out of your truck when you pulled up. We were all watching you. You were alone. No one got out.'

'Eh?' said the driver. 'Eh? No one with me?' And like a crumpling coat he slid down into the mud.

# Refugees' Christmas

*Phillip Allcock, a Monmouthshire artist of some note, reminisces with some friends about their wartime Christmases as evacuees. The Rolls Hall mentioned was founded by Charles Rolls, of Rolls Royce, which family were local to Monmouth. It now serves as the town library.*

We travelled by charabanc from Birmingham to see our brothers and sisters who had been evacuated to Monmouth. After visiting the houses where they were billeted and spending several happy hours with them, we all gathered, on Christmas Eve, at the Rolls Hall in Monmouth: the

parents, the children, the hosts and dignitaries, and the headmasters and teachers from the various schools in Birmingham.

The headmaster of St Mary's, Birmingham, Tom O'Laughlin, had organized a concert for the evening at the Rolls Hall, given by the children. There were a few sketches, recitation and community singing – even a demonstration of boxing done by the Birmingham boys and the local talent!

Either the weather or other factors kept us visitors in Monmouth overnight – some were able to sleep locally, but most of us slept on the floor of the Rolls Hall.

On Christmas morning we breakfasted on Christmas cake and cold custard, the remains of the supper from the night before. Delicious!

*A friend of Phillip's was evacuated to the Monmouth area at the same time.*

I was evacuated 1 September 1939 to Dinglestow Court as the guests of Mr and Mrs Bosanquet. I think he was a judge and she used to broadcast on diets. Then we were all rounded up in Monmouth town when the more permanent evacuation accommodation and schools had been sorted out.

So I spent the first Christmas of the war, in 1939, as an evacuee in Monmouth. My older brother, myself and two younger sisters were billeted with a family in a house near Monnow Bridge; the house no longer exists.

It was Christmas Eve, we three girls were whispering and giggling in anticipation of what surprises tomorrow would bring, remembering other Christmases, and the magic of it all. We hung up our stockings at the foot of the bed.

Christmas morning dawned, and we found our stockings just as we had left them – empty!

Diving under the bedclothes we wept.

On going downstairs, I cannot clearly recall what gifts there were, there are recollections of some sweets being wrapped in pretty paper and divided amongst us, and a few games and small items.

I am sure our family sent us what they could. We were a large family and very close. I know we received their love and thoughts.

Our teachers reminded us that, 'Wasn't there a war on?' – and we should accept that things would not be the same, and to learn to do

without and make the best of things, and to pray for those less fortunate than ourselves. Our childish minds could not comprehend that anything could be worse than empty stockings at Christmas.

The war was, to us, a long way away; our lives were full of adventure and new experiences, exploring the lovely countryside and the river and woods. Away from all the strife and bombings in the Midlands – and yes, we *did* make the best of it all; in a strange way, we felt 'special' as evacuees.

Perhaps in retrospect these were the 'gifts' we received that Christmas: we learned fortitude – to be strong in adversity – and to count our blessings. We were the lucky ones after all.

*Bridget Wadley lives just outside Monmouth: she also remembers that first Christmas.*

When asked to write on the subject, it surprised me that I could recall that first Christmas Day of the Second World War.

I was billeted with a lovely family in Rolls Avenue, Monmouth, and had spent a happy autumn exploring the countryside. For a ten-year-old girl, from the heart of Birmingham, this was paradise. But Christmas was drawing near and thoughts of home of course. There were times when I missed them all.

Christmas came, and on that morning I must have slept late, for daylight was streaming through the curtains, and at the bottom of my bed I found my stocking with nuts and an orange and chocolate money. There was also a pillowslip filled with a cardboard sweet shop, a pair of fur gloves, a scarf and some books. Once I was up and washed, I had breakfast before setting off for church.

When we came out of church we made our way to the Rolls Hall, where friends and relatives were waiting. I knew that there wouldn't be any of my relatives present; they were coming the following day. So, after seeing my two brothers, who were fostered with other families, I wandered off back to my foster home.

Although I can't say that I didn't enjoy my first Christmas of the war, I can remember feeling odd – not unhappy – but not being able to put my finger on it, with none of my own family around. But Boxing Day brought Mum, and that was lovely.

And so for the rest of my time as an evacuee, Christmas each year always had that strange feeling of not 'belonging'.

# Christmas on the Kitchen Front

*Christmas was a great problem for the housewife, with most foods rationed, and queues for everything else; many would save items all through the year. A bit of dried fruit one week, some tinned fruit the next; her collection of useful recipes would grow too. The Ministry of Food published many leaflets giving seasonal 'best buys', and there were a number of food experts and chefs who were very prolific at this time.*

A few of the most popular wartime cookbooks published to help the housewife 'make-do-and-mend'. (Private collection)

*Ambrose Heath had cookery books on everything from tinned foods and unrationed foods to packed lunches and leftovers in the larder. Many of these wartime cookery books had cartoon covers by Fougasse, to keep the kitchen cheerful in adversity! Here are a few typical Christmas recipes, which a wartime housewife would be able to achieve, ration coupons permitting, taken from these wartime books, and from housewives, who developed a trick or two of their own! Magazines such as* Good Housekeeping *did much to keep morale high on the Kitchen Front, and to advise housewives of the best way to make do, as in this morale booster from the Christmas issue, probably around 1940.*

# Keep up the Christmas Tradition

Once again the Christmas message of good cheer is heard, and the staff of *Good Housekeeping* institute offer readers greetings and best wishes. We hope that so far as wartime conditions permit you will all have a happy festival, and we hope too that you will be able to extract some enjoyment from your Christmas cooking and catering, even though it will probably present you with extra difficulties and problems this year. Even if you have to manage without this or that ingredient, there are substitutes to hand, if you are prepared to exercise intelligence and ingenuity.

In the ordinary way you would probably have prepared your puddings and cakes already, but cooking fats being rationed and other ingredients short or difficult to obtain this year, mixtures will be plainer and so cannot be expected to keep so well. We have therefore waited until this month to publish recipes.

It is difficult to say, as we write, what the exact position will be regarding the supply of suet when this article is published, but the abnormally big demand which is to be anticipated at Christmas time may lead to individual difficulties in obtaining supplies for puddings. We are therefore giving you a recipe for an economical pudding in which almost any cooking fat, such as margarine or dripping can be used instead of suet.

Eggs also must be cut down, but if you have dried eggs these can be mixed with water to replace fresh ones. Dried fruit will probably be reasonably plentiful, but you may have to substitute one kind for another. If, however, you embark on your cooking prepared to contrive in this way, there is no reason why your Christmas dinner should suffer.

# Wartime Menus

The menu *Good Housekeeping* recommends for the average household is:

> Roast chicken and sausages with roast potatoes and curly kale
> Scotch dumpling and custard sauce
> Mince pies, dessert and coffee.

Not bad in the circumstances! And the better-off menu is hardly different from today's:

> Roast turkey with chestnut stuffing with roast potatoes
>   and Brussels sprouts
> Christmas pudding with brandy butter
> Simple trifle with mock cream
> Dessert and coffee.

That the brandy butter is more likely to be brandy margarine, and the coffee made with acorns or dandelion root is all part of the big morale boost.

Morale boosts apart, what did the average family sit down to at Christmas? From our investigations, few were fortunate enough to have turkey – as one man put it 'all the trimmings maybe, but without the turkey'!

Let's start with the Christmas cake; for many, the only thing they managed to save coupons for. Many of the wartime cakes were plain spice cakes with a handful of fruit. Elaborate cardboard covers were made, and decorated to look like iced cakes. Very pretty on the table, and also kept the cake, which was served in small slices to last that bit longer, clean and moist underneath. But Stork Margarine (Van den Bergs) published a wartime cookery book which had something just a bit special for servicemen coming home for Christmas, or indeed to send to the men in the forces. A long-keeping cake iced with the symbols of the Army, the Navy or the Air Force. Expensive on coupons, but for many families, it was a way to show their loved ones how much they cared. The traditional moist Christmas cake recipe was then covered with icing made from blue dyed icing with a darker blue for waves (for the senior service); coffee essence coloured the icing to a

khaki colour for the Army, and a white icing with the coloured RAF wings emblem for the Air Force.

The Ministry of Food (MOF) in 1942 published a leaflet with a delicious recipe for stuffed mutton, fruit pies, Christmas pudding and emergency cream which was remarkably effective.

McDougall's published a heart-warming recipe for a sugarless **Christmas pudding** in 1940:

> ½ lb McDougall's SR flour
> 1 teaspoonful each spice and cinnamon
> ¼ teaspoonful each salt and nutmeg
> ½ lb breadcrumbs
> ½ lb shredded suet
> ½ lb each currants and sultanas
> ¼ lb mixed peel
> 6 oz chopped dates
> 1 large cooking apple grated
> 1 large carrot grated
> 6 oz treacle or syrup or honey
> 4 eggs
> 1½ gill milk, 1 gill brandy (optional)

Mix all together, put into greased basins and cover, then steam for five hours.

For a Christmas Eve supper, the MOF leaflet for December 1942 suggested **Hampton pie**

> ½lb cooked sausages
> ½ gill milk
> Tablespoonful mustard
> 1 onion chopped and fried
> 1 dessertspoonful parsley
> 2 tablespoonfuls ketchup
> Mashed potato to cover

Slice the sausage, mix with parsley, ketchup, mustard and stock. Arrange sausage in layers alternating with fried onion rings. Cover with mashed potato and bake in hot oven. That would have served two adults.

McDougall's cheerful Christmas advertisement for sugarless Christmas pudding.
(Private collection)

For the children, the MOF tried very hard at Christmas to create something for a treat – and in those days treats *were* treats! One housewife who kept a wartime recipe and household hints book, had an MOF leaflet with a recipe for **cinnamon drops**, to which she adds the note that, 'tied up in twists of paper, these make pretty take-home gifts after a tea-party, or to put in the stocking.'

> 5 teaspoonfuls ground cinnamon
> 8 oz sugar
> ¼ pint water.

Mix the cinnamon with the sugar, add the water and stir over a gentle heat until the sugar is dissolved, then boil rapidly without stirring until the crack stage (use a jam thermometer). That is, when dropped in cold water, mixture hardens immediately. For this quantity allow twenty minutes. Drop in small pieces from the point of a knife on to a greased plate and leave to harden.

This same housewife has a recipe for wartime toffee, using 2 oz sugar, 4 oz syrup, 2 teaspoonfuls bicarbonate of soda. Boil sugar and syrup together and add bicarb; stir quickly and put on to greased dish. No doubt this was a special treat for either her own children or perhaps if she was in charge of a children's home or school, and made these things for the children in her charge. Her recipe book is full of such delights, but sadly she left no record of her name. The book ends abruptly with only a few pages used.

One of the last entries is for **gingerbread men**, 'To put in the top of the stockings'.

> 2 oz sugar or syrup
> 2 oz margarine
> 8 oz plain flour
> ½ teaspoonful spice
> 2 teaspoonfuls ginger
> 1 level teaspoonful bicarb and lemon juice.

Melt syrup, sugar and margarine in a bowl, add a little flour, spice and lemon. Beat until smooth. Dissolve bicarb in a tablespoonful of tepid water and allow to cool. Then add the flour to mixture, blending

to a stiff dough. Knead until smooth. Make head, body, arms and legs and stick together with egg. Add currants for eyes.

Having had the chicken, if they were lucky, or the mock goose or stuffed mutton (basically the same thing!) with root vegetables, and a small portion of pudding and custard or mock cream for Christmas dinner, most families amused themselves by playing games until tea-time. This meal was not usually a collation between lunchtime and dinner as it is now, but during the war years was served about 6 p.m., and served as a supper, so Christmas Day tea-time was fairly substantial by the order of the day. Bread and margarine, or perhaps a little lemon curd made with dried egg, a few ounces of margarine and sugar and orange or lemon. This would make one jar, which spread thinly, could serve about eight people at a sitting, or last throughout the week!

**Cheese tartlets** were served hot or cold and consisted of short paste cases with a filling made from 2 oz breadcrumbs, 2 oz grated ends of cheese, 1 dried egg and 1 oz margarine, salt, pepper, milk and a pinch of baking-powder. This quantity in 4 oz pastry was supposed to suffice for four servings, according to the Ministry of Food.

Syrup was a little easier to get than sugar, so **ginger snaps**, made with 2 oz margarine, 1 tablespoonful sugar and 2 of syrup, 2 oz plain flour and a teaspoonful of ginger, were very popular for special occasions such as Christmas tea. Cooked for ten minutes and then rolled over a wooden spoon handle, this quantity made eighteen biscuits. There were no worries of overdoing the calories at least! The Christmas cake, if they were lucky, was served with a sliver of cheese.

# A Wink for the Butcher

ANGELA HUBERT

*The following extract from* Memories of Christmas Passed and Past, *brings home clearly how the sense of continuity on two fronts, was spoilt by the effects of the war. The background to the story begins before the First World War, but we pick it up in the 1920s, continuing through the Second World War to include the story of the infamous liquid paraffin sponge cake – a 'regular' favourite!*

For us, the highlight of the waiting time for Christmas was the parcel from Düsseldorf, which my father's godmother and her spinster sisters had been filling over the months for her beloved godson and his family.

My English grandmother had gone to a German finishing school in north Germany in the 1860s, to study the violin, and had made a lifelong friendship with the three Otterbein sisters, Maria, Gertrude and Gustel.

Despite the tragedy of the First World War, the bond had not been severed, and these three devoted women had continued to write to my grandmother and my father.

Every September, a letter would arrive from Tante Maria, asking for a list of things that we three little girls would most like for Christmas. I remember one year receiving a beautiful ring with an aquamarine in it.

Besides these individual gifts, there were always gorgeous marzipan fruits, gingerbread 'Hansel and Gretel' houses, and a large salami sausage for my father.

Tante Gertrude, bless her, always knitted warm, woolly knickers for us, which had to be worn with cotton linings, otherwise we would have scratched ourselves to death!

In 1933 my two sisters and I came down to Christmas morning breakfast wearing beautiful hand-knitted Bavarian jackets in black, red and green wool, with a row of little silver buttons down the front.

Alas, the bitterness of another war between us and Germany finally killed this generous and beautiful friendship, and the correspondence between my mother and those three good old sisters withered and died. Another casualty of war.

Even the hardships of food rationing during and after the conflict never prevented our family from celebrating Christ's birthday.

Our Christmas pudding and mince pies were made with great solemnity and pleasure from dried fruit which had been obtained from carefully-saved ration book 'points' and a predominance of carrots, breadcrumbs and apples. My mother always told me, the eldest, to go and flash my eyes at the local butcher for a piece of precious beef suet which was grated into the Christmas pudding mixture! It's strange how these memories come back after all these years.

One of the horrors of war was dried egg! I remember as a bride sitting with my husband in the back row of a cinema in Ipswich, eating chocolate together with those Horlicks tablets which were issued to aircrew – sheer bliss! One of those Ministry of Food short

films came on with 'Mrs Wartime Housewife' describing how to make an omelette from dried egg. When she came to the part where she described how tasty and nourishing it was, an American airman, smoking a cigar with his feet on the back of the seat in front, took out his cigar and shouted: 'It's a lie!'

So that we shouldn't suffer the indignities of dried egg, my mother kept chickens. We had a surfeit of eggs, but a shortage of everything else. We used to have an open house for young servicemen. After a while, our home was nicknamed 'The Patcham YMCA'. My mother used to garner various odds and ends, together with 'liberated' contributions from our various visitors; she used to employ these eggs in a variety of ways.

One festive addition was a Victoria sponge cake, made up with all those eggs, but deficient in either butter or margarine. My mother substituted liquid paraffin! It worked very well, but we noticed that one of our regular Canadian visitors became very 'regular' indeed. He seemed to spend a great deal of time in our lavatory. When my mother mentioned it to our local pharmacist, all manner of dire warnings were issued about leaching minerals from our systems; so no more sponges!

When I married my Polish airman in 1944 I became aware that from mid-November, if he had obtained leave, he became almost entirely engulfed in a thick fog of Slavonic gloom.

After many loving and bewildered questions, which were met with, 'You wouldn't understand, Aniuska', I found out that he, poor lad, was remembering with pained nostalgia, the Christmases he had enjoyed with his family in south-east Poland before he had been transported to a Siberian labour camp.

Gradually we evolved our own Christmas Eve celebrations, a mixture of Polish tradition and family ritual which survives to this very day. Hay spread under the white tablecloth to commemorate the Christ-child's lowly crib, and the Christmas wafer broken among us – a portion offered to everyone present, and saved for those loved ones not able to be together with the family. A loving personal wish and a kiss; hurts are healed, resentments, if any, melt away and the loving bonds are renewed through this lovely old Polish custom.

Would that wars could melt away so easily!

# Gert and Daisy's Cheap Christmas Pud

*Many still remember the radio broadcasts of Gert and Daisy Waters. Here is an extract from their first cookery book, entitled, appropriately, Gert and Daisy's Wartime Cookery Book! This little book found its way into many kitchens in those days of limited groceries and tight budgets. They dedicated their book to 'The Officers, Warrant Officers and Men of the Royal Navy and Merchant Navy, not forgetting the lads of the fishing fleets, all of whom risk their lives so that we may eat our daily bread.'*

Dear Girls,

This is our first cookery book, and it was written at the request of many of you who didn't switch us off when we did our 'Feed the Brute' talks on the wireless.

You will find the recipes very easy to do, and as cheap as we can make them, and although we know they are good old 'tried and trues' we hope that one or two of them will be new to one or two of you.

Now don't forget the salt and pepper – you don't want everything to taste like a bit of flannel – and if you can treat yourselves to the few simple herbs we have used in the directions they will only cost you a few pence, last you a long time, and if you expect the dish to taste the same without them you'll find it won't.

Don't forget to make the meals look as nice as you can – there's all the difference between a meal that's nicely dished up and one that's chucked at you, because, as the old song says, 'It's not the bit of fish, it's the parsley round the dish that tickles the poor old man!'

We've been attending the cookery demonstrations that have been got up for us all, all over the country, and we were glad to see so many of you there as well. It only goes to show that you're not too stuck up to learn something new, and, in any case, it's a change from the pictures – it rests your eyes, don't it?

We will now close, hoping it finds you all well as it leaves us at present, and we'll wish you the best of luck and a safe journey to you

and yours wherever it may be, always bearing in mind that stormy days don't last for ever, and that one day the sun will shine again.

Love from all to all,

Your loving friends,

Gert and Daisy

Now here's something for your Christmas stores: **cheap Christmas pudding**. If there's one pudding above all others that we look forward to, children and grown-ups too, it's a Christmas pudding, and so we are going to give you a recipe for a cheap one in these hard times.

Talking about Christmas pudding, old Bert bought one once in a second-hand shop. It cost him fourpence, and Daisy didn't 'arf lead off at him for wasting fourpence on a second-hand Christmas pudding; but as it turned out, Bert was on the right side of the laugh, 'cos he found fourteen threepenny bits in it. As we don't suppose you'll be able to have the same sort of luck, 'cos after all, them things only happen once in a while, like measles, here's the way to make:

### Cheap Christmas pudding

½ lb flour (8 heaped tablespoonfuls)

½ lb breadcrumbs (16 heaped tablespoonfuls)

½ lb suet (8 heaped tablespoonfuls)

¼ lb dates (cut up)

¼ lb prunes (cut up)

4 level tablespoonfuls raisins

4 level tablespoonfuls sultanas

4 level tablespoonfuls currants

½ lb grated carrots

2 oz candied peel

½ lb apples, chopped

1 nutmeg

1 teaspoonful spice

1 lemon, rind and juice

¼ lb sugar (4 level tablespoonfuls)

½ lb treacle

1 tumblerful milk and water mixed

Mix all together and steam for eight hours, or boil for six hours

beforehand, and three on Christmas Day. This quantity is enough to fill two medium size basins. (NB Two eggs may be added if you like, but it's a very good pudding without them.)

In case you have a bit of a party, we're going to give you recipes for extra-specials: **orange cream**

> 1 orange jelly
> 1 orange
> 1 small tin unsweetened milk (6½*d* size)

Add the juice of the orange and enough hot water to make half a pint instead of the usual pint. Stir until the jelly has dissolved. Whisk up the evaporated milk till thick and frothy like soapsuds, stir in the jelly and whisk again; pour into a glass dish. This sets very quickly and when it is set you can decorate it with slices of orange.

# The Rezepte of Fräulein Oberländer: A Mystery for Christmas!

*The last few German Jews to escape Hitler's 'ethnic cleansing' were still getting out of Germany and Austria right up to the beginning of the war. Many held on in the hopes that all would be well. Others needed to sell their homes and businesses in order to have something to escape with, often selling at a third of the value. Many were reluctant to leave elderly parents, too infirm to be able to take the rough journeys which faced them. One such was Else Oberländer. She escaped to Britain, leaving her parents behind, with only her mother's recipe book, begun in 1919, to give her comfort. The book also contained letters. The following is dated May 1939.*

Dear Fräulein Oberländer,
I was very glad to have your letter, and I do hope you will be able to leave without any bother. Mrs Essinger will meet you at the station and bring you to the house. Hoping to see you soon,
I am,
Yours sincerely,
C.M. Watson.

Had she got a position as a cook in an English household? Was this why her mother's parting gift was her treasured cookery book? We shall never know. All we do know is that she did arrive safely in England, and her mother's book continued to be filled with recipes, first written in German, and all wartime economy, then in a strange half-English, half-German mixture, and finally in English. German Christmas cookies give way to wartime recipes for Christmas pudding without egg, custard made with dried egg, and mincemeat without sugar, and a delicious and simple recipe, passed on by her mother, for **apple sponge**:

First cook some apples. Melt 2 oz butter (or margarine), put 2 oz sugar in, stir well. Add two dried eggs and four heaped tablespoonfuls self-raising flour. Mix with some milk to drop from spoon (dropping consistently). Cook on greased baking sheet as sponge drops, or as a cake in a tin.

Her parents mercifully survived the Holocaust, whether they stayed in Germany or moved elsewhere we do not know, but letters came from both parents in 1948 – still with new recipes! – and in 1955, Fräulein Oberländer had moved to Weston-super-Mare, and received mail from Israel.

Fräulein Oberländer's book contained not only her own and her mother's recipes, but a number of pasted-in pages from wartime magazines and papers, with particular emphasis on the Christmas issues – with recipes, home hints, stories and features which obviously appealed to her. It is from these that the following extracts are taken.

HINTS FOR THE HOME COOK from *Woman's Weekly*:
When nutmegs become too small to grate, do not throw them away – put the pieces into the peppermill with the peppercorns. The ground nutmeg and pepper blend together very nicely.

Asparagus rolls are a favourite party savoury, but equally nice are celery rolls. Choose the small heart part of the celery and cut it into dainty lengths. Cut the bread and margarine thinly and remove all crusts so that the bread will roll smoothly. Roll the celery in the bread and margarine, and serve with small dices of cheese. Don't forget to save the crusts for another use.

SHELTER COMFORT from *Good Housekeeping*'s 'Christmas Gift Guide':
Your friends who are economizing with makeshift furnishings for their cellar or Anderson shelter would be delighted to receive any of the gifts

## Shelter Comfort

**Your friends who are economising with makeshift furnishings for their cellar or "Anderson" would be delighted to receive any of the practical gifts shown here**

Above, left : The roll-up mattress is very soft and comfortable to lie on, and light to carry. The waterproof underside is a practical feature ; the top is covered with gay chintz in a choice of colourings. The light, inexpensive camp bed is designed for shelter use, but will also be invaluable for putting up an additional visitor during the Christmas holidays. Harrods

With the sirens starting so early each evening, we predict many picnic meals throughout this winter, and a basket containing two thermos jars, cups, etc., will make it easy to serve hot soup, coffee, tea, etc. Harrods

Left : Two suggestions for " shelter-sleepers " or friends in the services: A sleeping bag filled with tropal, which is claimed to be much warmer than wool; it fastens at the side with a zipp, and rolls up and straps neatly for carrying ; and an all-wool three-layer sleeping bag, a real bargain at 39s. 6d. Harrods

Lighting is a problem, but here are three suggestions to solve it : (1) A battery lamp which is also useful for carrying in the blackout. (2) A miniature oil lamp, obtainable in pink, blue or green, costing 2s. 3d. Both from Peter Jones, Ltd. (3) Candles are fashionable again, and this pottery candlestick in pretty colourings costs 2s. 11d. Gorringes

Shelter comforts. *Good Housekeeping*'s practical gift guide for Christmas 1940.
(Private collection)

shown here. The roll-up mattress is very soft and comfortable to lie on and light to carry. The waterproof underside is a practical feature and the top is covered in gay chintz. The light, inexpensive camp bed is designed for shelter use, but will also be invaluable for putting up an additional visitor during the Christmas holidays. From Harrods.

With the sirens starting so early each evening, we predict many picnic meals throughout this winter. A basket containing two thermos flasks, cups etc. will make it easy to serve hot drinks and soups.

Lighting is a problem, but here are some suggestions to solve it: a battery lamp which is also useful for carrying in the blackout; a miniature oil-lamp obtainable in pink, blue or green costing 2*s* 3*d*. [about 11p], available from Peter Jones.

THE SHELTER CAKE from *Good Housekeeping*, Christmas 1940:
The Anderson shelter is a byword with most of us now and makes an amusing and topical subject for a cake, especially if there are children in the family.

Bake the cake mixture in an oblong mould or small bread tin and allow to cool, then cover each side with a layer of marzipan, cutting a small 'door' out of the front piece. Next, cut and fix a piece right over the top, marking corrugations with a skewer. Gather the trimmings and knead in enough cocoa to make the colour of earth, and bank them up against the sides of the shelter. Finally, cover with a layer of snow made by melting 6–8 white marshmallows and pouring over. Leave a clearing in front of the 'shelter' for a path and sprinkle with finely-chopped burnt almonds to imitate gravel.

# A Medal for Mrs Smith

*While their menfolk were suffering such dreadful front line conditions, wives, mothers and sweethearts suffered no less the agonies of being 'stuck at home', often without their children even to care for; working long hours in ammunition factories, or in the Land Army, 'gardening for Britain'. They had to provide meals from nothing, make clothes last for years – a great difficulty with growing children – and cope with awful depressions. Many of the middle classes were managing for the first time without*

*domestic help, which was common in the smallest household up to the war.
They could not cook, sew, budget – and suddenly they had to do all that
and work too. These women were fighting a war as much, in their own
way, as their menfolk were in theirs, and it is to these that the following
words from the editor of* Good Housekeeping *were aimed.*

Mrs Smith doesn't mention medals when she writes to her soldier
husband. She has no medals to mention. Housewives don't get visible
decorations for bravery: their medals are worn very quietly, in their
own immediate circle, in a few people's hearts.

But Second Lieutenant Smith, serving somewhere in the desert,
wears his wife's colours proudly. He knows the job she is doing. Not all
the details of it of course – he just thinks of it as 'carrying on'. He
doesn't remember that her domestic help has gone long since and that
the daily helps who oblige grow less obliging every day. He doesn't
know that shopping could take a good half of every week now, if she
lets it; but she doesn't, because cooking, cleaning, looking after the
children, gardening and tending the chickens all have to share her time
too. He hasn't heard much about her civil defence duties, her knitting,
her regular salvage hunts and the mathematics wartime housekeeping
entails.

Mathematics? That subaltern in the desert would smile if he could
see his wife in the evenings now. Busy with pencil and paper working
out the points, figuring out her fuel target, adding up her last winter's
coal bills. . . . Brave Mrs Smith, who 'always hated figures'. She really
does deserve a medal for that.

Fortitude, valour, gallantry. Fine words when they are used to
describe fine deeds; but they apply equally well to every British
housewife today. There's a special fortitude about keeping the home
fires burning on a minimum of fuel, and gallantry is extra gallant when
it has to be practised from seven till ten every day.

*Good Housekeeping* humbly offers Mrs Smith its compliments, and
would like to give her all the medals there are. Meanwhile, if the
Institute can help her in any possible way – with facts or figures or
advice or tested recipes – *Good Housekeeping* will be only too glad.

# Christmas on the Home Front

*How did people manage to celebrate Christmas despite the privations and dangers of the war? These accounts are typical of many.*

## Christmas on the Farm

### MRS WRIGGLESWORTH

We had a big dairy and mixed farm. I was a young bride at the beginning of the war, and shared my husband's farm with his mother and father, an aunty whose husband had gone to war, and several nephews and nieces from the rest o' t' family what lived in places like Leeds, and even up in Newcastle. Family evacuees I suppose really, but charity begins at 'ome so they say! We also had three little 'uns from Lunden – a stout little fella of twelve who'd promised to look after 'is sisters, so much so 'e'd tied them to him wi' string so they couldn't be separated! They were left till last 'cos no one wanted to tek three together.

They all loved it! They 'ad to work mind, no room for guests on a farm wi' most of t' menfolk gone to war! There was cows to be milked – all be hand – poultry to see to, pigs down the lane to be scrubbed out. We allus limewashed all t' building afore Kerstemus, so all t' youngsters were dressed up in owld overalls, wi' scarves or caps on theer heads, and given a bucket an' brush each. The littlest only 'ad whitewash wi' a dollybag in to mek it blue – the flies doan't like blue see – an' limewash can burn.

Kerstemus were allus good, war or no, there was allus surplus produce we could use to us own. We had a big Kerstemus tree as well, right up t' ceiling it were, an' 'cos we was in a place reckoned to be

*45*

safe, we weren't afear'd to put us best baubles on. Weslyn balls of shiny glass, little glass birds wi' spunglass tails, little Faither Kerstemus figures med from crêpe paper an' pipecleaners, an' strands of silvery stuff, like lametta today, but heavy, wi' tin or mebbe lead in it. The little 'uns would have first bash, wi' loads o' cotton wool to brush on to t' branches, an' sprinkle wi' glitterdust, then they were told that it had to be left for Faither Kerstemus to finish off. 'Ee it were a nice job, late on Kerstemus Eve, decoratin' the tree, wi' a drop of parsnip wine to add merryment to t' proceedings!

One year during t' war we had twenty-two stockings to fill! It were mostly sweets and biscuits an' apples. Knitted socks and stockings, an' Grandad were champion at whittlin', so there were wooden animals, and peg dollies, an' tops for walking sticks for t' older lads. We 'ad the 'three musketeers', as we called them from Lunden, for three years. They were champion little farm-hands by t' time we'd finished wi' em! They even cried when it were time to go 'ome! Kem back every year for the summer they did, an' helped out. Jack ended up marryin' a local lass in 1950.

For us dinner we 'ad chicken and pork. We also had a big 'am, basted in treacle, nice it were. An' we allus med a big standin' pie wi' hot water pastry, nice and stiff so it stood up alone, an' held the meat inside. We'd mek a jelly stock with boiled down pig's feet and bits like that; it turned to jelly when it were cold, and was a good way of filling up corners in the pies. There was allus loads o' pickles and preserves, even durin' t' war – all fruit an' little sugar, but better for you for a' that. We'd 'ave a bit o' spice cake – yule loaf Mam-in-law called it – an' mint pasty. That were med wi' currants (we use' t' use dried elderberries a lot), mixed wi' chopped mint an' a bit o' sugar if it were spared, all mixed together wi' a bit o' butter, an' spread on a pastry bed, then another square o' pastry on top, an' baked in t' oven, then cut into squares. Popular that were.

We allus 'ad a big cheese to go wi' the yule loaf an' spice cakes, an' the apple pies that Mam baked by the dozen for Kerstemus! She needed to wi' all us lot. We'd listen to the King's message, an' then play games like hide and seek – there were a lot of right good places to 'ide on the farm I can tell you. Even a secret slope under a step that went down to t' cellar!

Not all the little vaccy's 'ad such a good time. We 'ad one in '41 who was covered in sores all over 'er bum. The place she were at made 'er

wash 'er own smalls, an' she would put them on 'alf wet 'cos there was no drying in the room. She were skin an' bone, honestly. But we soon put that right! Plenty of good creamy milk an' Mam's spice biscuits an' she were fine. She stayed wi' us until the end of the war; her house was done in in the blitz, an' 'er Mam were working in service to get some brass together, so we kept Mavis on. We weren't wealthy, but we worked hard and played hard. We were the lucky ones during them war years. We only read about the awful things that 'appened in the cities like Leeds, an' Manchester an' Lunden. We was lucky so we shared us fortune wi' a few as wasn't so, well, you do don't you.

# Deck the Shelters with Paper Garlands

*A family remembers trying to decorate and prepare for Christmas during the blitz. Their sheer determination to have a traditional Christmas come what may was the stuff the British home front was made of; a stoic determination not to take any notice of the bombs!*

We had always had a big tree, a real one. My uncle had a small farm, and we always got one from him; it was his present to us every year. So we had lots of lovely glass decorations, mostly from before the First World War, that had belonged to my grandfather's sister. She had married a German glassblower from Thuringia. Lovely they were, little glass birds, and Father Christmases, a cuckoo clock, and balls of all sizes and colours.

We also had a Christmas tree made from goose feathers. Not that you'd know they were feathers, they were processed – another German secret! But a good one.

It was this feather tree that was our saving during the war. It was only three feet tall, and in its own little wooden pot. So we used to decorate it with all non-breakable things, like tinsel stars, pipecleaner animals and suchlike, and paper things and tinsel. Then we could pick it up and take it down into the shelter with us! All the lovely old glass decorations were carefully wrapped and taken down to my uncle's for safety. We still have most of them.

Women employees decorating a Christmas tree on one of the London underground stations. (London Transport Museum)

I was one of three sisters and two brothers, and we lived within the sound of Bow bells, though our family came from Wales and north of London, and were country folk. Our Mam was one of twelve! Catholics – big families; very useful in times of war, a nuisance the rest of the time!

We managed to have a Christmas Mass in the cellars of the church in 1942. All candlelit, and completely blacked out, it was like it must have been hundreds of years ago. We got a real sense of continuity there. I remember there were no Communion wafers, so we had stale bread consecrated instead! It felt funny chewing Holy Communion as we'd always been taught not to touch the wafer with your teeth but to let it dissolve. The nuns who made the wafer hosts had used up all their flour supply, having given it to one of the local lads. He had been in a seminary, but had left to serve his country in the Army before he was made priest. As he was a deacon, he had got special permission to take Holy Communion to the front line troops fighting Rommel in Africa. So the nuns had supplied him with all their flour at short notice, as those poor lads never got a chance to even see a church.

The priest talked about pulling together and helping each other and those who needed our help. War certainly does something to bring communities closer together. Mind, we always were close in the East End. It's all changed now. Not much of the old East End spirit left.

# A Farmhouse Christmas in London's Blitz

*Flo, the eldest sister of the family in the previous extract, who was married with a young family, lost her home with a direct hit, and spent Christmas with her grandmother. Now eighty-one she positively sparkles with the memory of, what was for her, a magical opportunity that would not have occurred had it not been for the war – several years spent getting to know grandparents, who had been rather shadowy figures up until then.*

Gran had a big house; five bedrooms, eight steps leading up to the front door, and a huge cellar, which Grandpa had used as a workshop; he was a carpenter by trade. They brought up twelve children in that house. I suppose it didn't seem so big with all that lot, but with just

the two of them it was a wonderful temporary home for me and the kids, especially with my husband away.

Anyway, we cleared away Grandpa's stuff in the cellar, and made quite a cosy den down there. Grandpa knocked up two sets of bunks for the kids in their own corner, and another set for him and Gran. I had a cosy little hole done like they used to have in Wales, where he'd been brought up with a sort of cupboard bed. We had a gas stove down there, but Gran preferred to use the old fired copper which Grandpa adapted for her. She wasn't happy about the gas being used. We spent most of our time down there during the blitz in fact. It got pretty dark though as Grandpa had blocked up the window with sandbags against blast. We had lots of Tilley lamps, as there never had been electricity or gas lamps down there, and Grandpa needed plenty of light for his work. We were luckier than most I reckon, with our shelter comforts.

Grandpa had, with the help of a couple of neighbours, put up four huge beams going across the cellar and resting on the top of the bare brick and stone walls – to give a bit of extra protection in case of a direct hit he said. My poor little two up, two down didn't stand a chance, but Gran's house was made of much sterner stuff!

We decorated properly for Christmas down there, with jolly paper streamers and honeycomb pendants. The kids made loads of paper garlands which we had put all over the house! It kept them occupied for hours – a pile of newspapers, a box of paints and thick brushes, scissors and some flour paste Gran made them.

We had a wireless down there too, rigged up with a wire through the floor above, and Gran and Grandpa had brought down their favourite comfy chairs. We had plenty of food too as Gran's stores were all down in the cellar in little walk-in cupboards with stone slabs and air holes to the outside for freshness. She was a great one for making all her own stores: dried and salted meat and fish, potted meats, pickled eggs, chutneys full of vitamins, jams, hundreds (it seemed like anyway) of kilner jars of preserved fruit and veg. She even had four 12 1b cheeses that she had got from her niece's farm in Buckinghamshire the previous year. So our Christmas 1940 was better than most, and she had stores to save for the leaner years to come.

Grandpa had this lovely musical revolving Christmas tree stand; it was German, of course. It was a silvery metal, very ornate, with a big key. You put a small feather tree in the hole at the top, and when it was wound up, the tree revolved to the tunes of 'Silent Night' and 'Von Himmel Hoch'.

Magical it was. On Christmas Eve the candles would be lit, and the stand wound up, and you should have seen the looks on the kids' faces.

The kids didn't miss much in the way of presents either, with Gran making sweets and dolls and knitted bonnets and Balaclavas, gloves, stockings and cardigans, and Grandpa making all manner of wooden things. That first year he made a Noah's ark, using all different bits of wood, so the animals didn't need any painting as they looked lovely in all their different texture and shades of natural wood. We still have one or two pieces of his work in the family, but children today don't appreciate that sort of thing as much. They should have been kept as a tribute to Grandpa really.

*from*

# Dear Merv – Dear Bill: 2

## MERVYN HAISMAN AND L.E. SNELLGROVE

1 December 1940 – . . . Christmas is coming but I'm not looking forward to it. Won't be as good as last year and in spite of the bombs I wish I could spend it at home. Your friend, Merv.

1 January 1941 – Dear Merv, Happy New Year! It seems ages since we last met and it's well over a month since I wrote to you. I had to go back and read your last letter to see if you'd written anything of great importance. Needn't have bothered. No, seriously though, thanks for your account of the bombing of Kenward Road. From now on, when I hear a bomb screaming down at me, I will comfort myself that you've told me it can't have my number on it. I only hope to God that your brother Eric is right!

Actually I didn't hear about your house being bombed until quite some time afterwards. I expect Churchill himself made sure no one

knew about it in case Mussolini started to get above himself. The fact that the Haisman family are still alive and well, will I'm sure, be a great disappointment to the Italian High Command.

I hope your Christmas wasn't as bad as you thought it was going to be, because you really sounded down in the dumps. Just to cheer you up I'll pass on some of your news to the girls. They even remembered you and a few – the blind and the stupid – wished you were back here. Probably want to get even with you for what you did to them at Deal!

I've heard that the school is going to open again this term, which means that in spite of all the slaughter and destruction, I shall only have lost one term. . . .

I think my memories of this Christmas will be of fog! Every time Dad and I went up to the baths it was foggy. I also said goodbye to Uncle Will in a thick fog just before Christmas. He was called up and came to say goodbye to Mum and Dad. Mum was very upset – after all he's her only brother – but Dad never did like him. He's a strange chap because no sooner had he arrived, than he took Mum and me off to the cinema. Afterwards, I offered to walk up the road with him. He was very pleased and thought that I was going because of him. I hadn't the heart to tell him I'd planned to see Smithson anyway. So we walked along in the freezing cold, and he was grateful, and I felt awful, as though I'd deceived him in some way. Being a romantic, I watched him disappear in the swirling fog thinking that it might be the last time (which it might!).

The Saturday before Christmas was memorable! I know that with you it's Sundays, but I now have a great liking for Saturdays! This is probably because of the description in Tom Sawyer of his delight at being free from school and being able to do what he wanted. I feel just the same.

Well, this particular Saturday was special because it was the last before Christmas. I cycled round Blackfen. It was cold, clear and bright – the fog having lifted – then I called on Smithson and suggested a game of tennis. Naturally the courts were closed and we climbed over the wire. It was a very funny feeling playing tennis on a winter's day with gloves on!

. . . I spent Christmas Eve at Smithson's house. We played whist with his parents and his father gave us some beer. He said it was a special sort. I don't know what it was, but I certainly could get to like it. I had quite a few and I left their house well after midnight, feeling

quite light-headed, and began singing at the top of my voice. Near the Yorkshire Grey I stumbled over a park bench, which I set over the tramlines so the trams could have some fun in the morning. Back home, I took my shoes off before I crept into the house. I'd seen so many drunks doing it in funny films it seemed the right thing to do. Then I played Father Christmas to Mum and Dad, which was a bit of a change round. After that, I staggered off to bed. In the morning when Dad came in to give me my present – a shirt – I had a really bad headache, which made Dad roar with laughter. He said, 'The first of many, come on, hair of the dog.' Then he took me to the Yorkshire Grey, where he was convinced I'd spent a wild evening. He bought me a brown ale and made me drink it. I drank it very slowly, feeling sick all the time. . . . Cheerio, Bill.

**9 January 1941** – Dear Bill, Thanks for your letter – it helped to cheer me up. I'm afraid that all of us are feeling a bit down in the dumps at the moment. Christmas wasn't as bad as I thought it was going to be. We had chicken for dinner – but of course, no sloe-gin this year. In the afternoon we were taken to the drawing room and had tea with the Griffiths, but no one played games or anything like that, so it was all a bit boring. . . .

We don't do so badly for food down here. I think Mrs Evans knows a poacher so we get a lot of rabbit, either stewed or roasted, which is my favourite. Of course, trying to get sweets is a waste of time. Oh yes, talking of food, have you ever had pheasant? Take a tip from me, don't bother. Some time before Christmas the Colonel had guests for dinner and Mrs Evans cooked pheasants' legs coated with mustard. There were a couple over and she asked me if I'd like a taste.

I had one mouthful and was nearly sick. The meat was rotten and really stank to high heaven. Mrs Evans said that was because it was well hung and had to be a bit 'high'. I wouldn't even give meat like that to a dog. Another thing, Stilton. It's a cheese and it smells like bad socks and has maggots crawling in it. I asked Mrs Evans if she was going to throw it away and she sounded quite shocked. 'Goodness gracious no, it's beautifully ripe.' I tell you Bill, if being rich means you have to eat food like that, I think I'll stay poor and live longer.

. . . Well that's about all that's been happening down here lately. As you can see, it's all a bit boring. Hope to have some brighter news in my next letter. Write soon, your friend, Merv.

*from*

# Harvest of Messerschmitts

## DENNIS KNIGHT

*In the following diary entries from Dennis Knight's book, chronicling a village at war in 1940, the airmen relate how they spent Christmas and New Year at the Kent village of Elham, on the Downs behind Folkestone and Dover.*

**23 December** – Still very cold. Churchill spoke to the Italian people at night. Captain Menzies, RA came to Elham from Regimental HQ and informed a rather depressed audience of officers and NCOs that a German invasion over the Christmas period was a distinct possibility.

**24 December** – Ran about with telegrams and presents all day. Jerry at night. No operations by our bombers. At Hawkinge the general decorating of the camp was ordered.

Christmas Eve was an extra special day at the vicarage, it being the birthday of both the vicar and his second daughter, Margaret, who was ten. During the sound of Big Ben before the BBC news broadcast at 9 p.m., the family remained still while the vicar said his customary evening prayer.

**25 December** – Christmas Day. Uncle and Miss Wellsted came to tea and dinner. Quiet all day. The King spoke on 'Christmas under fire'. The services' tradition on Christmas Day for the officers and NCOs to wait upon the men at their tables was observed at aerodromes and camps all over Britain. In some of the 'beer-ups' that followed, airmen and officers swapped jackets and jokes and differences in rank were forgotten for a few hours. Major Bassett contrived to have dinner with his men at both Elham and Lyminge.

In farms, cottages and urban houses, the civilians consumed goose,

duck or chicken, but in Mary Smith's home the day was blighted because her father was extremely ill. At 3 p.m. the wireless was switched on and the entire nation listened with respect to the faltering speech of King George VI. It had been an extraordinary year and neither the King nor his subjects quite realized that they had lived through 'their finest hour'.

**26 December** – Quite a good meet (East Kent foxhounds); a quiet foggy day.

615 squadron – Churchill's own – flew down from Kenley to spend the morning at Hawkinge. The East Kent Hunt always had their Boxing Day hunt meet at Elham village and despite bombing and food shortages, Major Wood and Freddie Sturmey had the hounds in good fettle (even though they were having to consume some of their horses). The Square and High Street were filled with riders and sightseers and the pubs were dispensing stirrup cups and noggins. In the evening a telegram arrived at the post office and Edward Smith insisted in getting up from his sick bed to deliver it personally.

The Royal Norfolk Hotel, Sandgate, had been granted an extension of their licence to sell drinks up until midnight and during the night a recreation train, pulled by a Dean goods locomotive, charged full tilt through the newly-repaired level crossing gates in Elham and continued on its way to Canterbury. Some say they could hear the sound of singing above the clamour as it passed.

**31 December** – That evening the people of Folkestone held a New Year's Eve Grand Spitfire Dance. The posters read:

BOBBY'S RESTAURANT
New Year's Eve

GRAND SPITFIRE DANCE AND CABARET
in aid of Folkestone Herald Spitfire Fund

Dancing to Bobby's Sweet Rhythm Orchestra
Extension 1 a.m. – Bars until 12.30 a.m.
Admission 2s  HM Forces 1s

Dinner – Light refreshments – Cold buffet

At midnight, as the dancers sang 'Auld Lang Syne', Folkestone was in darkness and there were no bells ringing in the New Year – just a few peeps on some ships' hooters in the darkened harbour. The proceeds of the dance, when added to the town's accumulated fund, were just about enough to pay for one more Spitfire.

# A Pre-Christmas Present – from Adolf!

### ARTHUR SCHOLEY

*Arthur Scholey is better known for his children's plays and stories rather than wartime memories, but here is a short contribution of a memory from Mr Scholey's own childhood during the war years.*

'Twas a night before Christmas (12/13 December 1940) that German bombers focused their attention on my then home town of Sheffield. I was eight, and remember being woken up by my parents as the sirens went and grabbing the bag of 'things to keep me occupied' – Plasticine, coloured pencils, paper, glue, scissors – before hurrying down to the reinforced cellar. This fascinated me, not least because of a newly-excavated mysterious tunnel, which now connected us with our neighbours and along which we, or they, would crawl in the event of a direct hit.

We all thought that direct hit had happened. The shattering explosion covered us with the dust of decades. Convinced that the bomb had landed in our backyard, I vividly recall my father eventually venturing out and clinging to the wall that divided our gardens, for fear that the black hole in the centre was in fact a crater.

Topical cartoon showing Hitler with a tree full of bombs and scrawny chickens –
his Christmas gift to the German people, Christmas 1942! (Private collection)

Dawn brought us relief from that – but also sorrow. The church had
had a direct hit. We hurried through broken glass and bricks. Two
walls only were standing, but on one of them the motto affirmed above
the ruins: 'O Worship the Lord in the Beauty of Holiness'.

A new church would arise – but that was a Christmas yet to come . . .

# A Welcome Visitor and the Manchester Blitz

*The blitz took its toll on Christmas, but the people were undaunted. The cinemas showed Pathé newsreels to strengthen the hearts of the most downhearted. Manchester cinema-goers, whose Christmas was blitzed in 1940, were treated to a visit from that grand old gent, Father Christmas, in this report.*

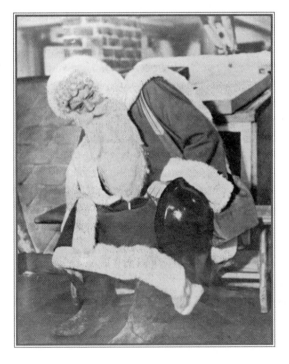

Even Father Christmas has his tin hat when trudging the streets during the blitz. (Christmas Archives)

Once upon a Christmas a very good man would come down the chimney. But this year he walks among the ruins of many homes, shaking his head sadly at the work of an evil being that nobody loves.

Hello, there goes the alert – you see the kiddies have organized their own spotting system. Into action go window watchers and chimney spotters. For Father Christmas has arrived. Soon the whole district is alive with excited boys and girls. Twelve whole months they have waited for this moment, mind you, they were beginning to wonder whether he had had a bomb on his place too. But here he is, the old darling, and his toys are not rationed!

He's soon surrounded by children and mothers with toddlers in arms, all pushing and eager to see what is in that bulging sack on his back. Mum and Dad were wrong when they said that there mightn't be a Father Christmas this year. At last, something to play with. A tin telephone box filled with sweets for the first, a spotted dalmation toy dog for a little girl, whose smile says more than a thousand words; and a model Spitfire plane for a solemn little boy of three or four, who is too young even to have ever remembered a peacetime Christmas.

Good old Santa Claus; coo Mum, now we can have a Christmas tree with lights on and everything – we mustn't forget the blackout though. Two children set up a wire Christmas tree in the window of their bombed-out home. A *6d* tinsel star from Woolworths goes on the top, and some cardboard ornaments with glass fibre rays. A little glass bird with a glass fibre tail. No lights here, but to those children it is the most beautiful tree in the world. It'll be a nice Christmas.

*And Manchester people remember their own Blitz experiences.*

# Reason to celebrate

MARIE MORAN

It was the time of the Manchester blitz and one night, just before 24 December, from a shelter on a hill some miles away, I had watched the blazing city, heart sick with the knowledge that somewhere amidst the dreadful conflagration were all my loved ones.

When morning came I set out to find them. A bus took me as far as the outer suburbs, but could go no further. From there I walked for miles, picking my way over broken glass, smouldering rubble, and hose-pipes. The streets were packed with people either driven from their homes or trying to get to work. Among all these crowds I suddenly came upon three of my sisters. They had spent the night in a shelter, but assumed that the rest of the family were safe.

Since they had eaten nothing since tea-time the previous day, we made our way to the city in the hope of finding a café. Some were open, but there was no water! Finally we found a rather battered milk bar, which had milk but no food. Luckily I had with me a large box of chocolates which had been sent from Ireland, and which I had collected the previous afternoon. So our lunch consisted of cold malted milk and 'Black Magic'!

Sometimes when I smell the Christmas turkey in the oven, I recall that festive meal! We were together – we had reason to celebrate!

# A 'Coronation Street' Christmas

## ELSIE HUGHES

I will always remember Christmas 1940. I was a young child and my brother was a baby at the time and he was teething. So off I went with my father to deliver Christmas presents to our relatives in Cheshire, while Mum stayed home with the baby.

On our return, as we neared Manchester, the whole sky was bright red; the blitz had begun, so we had to take shelter for the night. The following morning we made our way past heaps of rubble, where people's homes had stood. Smoke still filled the air. Happily our house was still intact apart from a few broken windows. Some of our neighbours were less lucky. As we were a close knit 'Coronation Street' type of community, we decided to pack all our food, toys and clothes so that everyone could share our Christmas. On Christmas Day our house was packed with people, and someone brought an accordian. The piano was wheeled out, and we all had a good old knees up.

Even to this day, people still talk about that wonderful Christmas. Perhaps it was because it caught the true meaning of Christmas – caring and sharing with those less fortunate than yourself.

# Christmas at Bryniau

## MARGARET MAXFIELD

*Having taken a fortnight's respite from wartime bombing at a remote*
*Welsh cottage, and deciding to stay, Margaret Maxfield writes about her*
*family's experiences of their first Christmas at the cottage.*

Our first Christmas at Bryniau still stands in my memory as most picturesque; there were holly trees at the back door, and the boys had done a splendid job of Christmas decorating. The porch had its bough and the walls their garlands. Our ancient cooking range 'Excelsior' was fuelled with logs that could boil, roast, or toast whatever our palates demanded. We even had snow to complete the picture in this remote cottage in the Welsh mountains which had suddenly become home to us.

We were able to share the festive season with relatives, all glad to have some respite from the bombing that Birmingham was suffering. Our 'refugees' consisted of my widowed mother-in-law, my widowed father, and a pretty young cousin – all glad of a break from the nightly fear of the bombing raids. They wanted a safe place with quiet nights. Bryniau had all that.

The two elders sat cosily each side of the fire, and a brass oil lamp which Gran had contributed, threw a warm glow over the room. It also blackened the ceiling with soot but we did not worry about such trifles. This was our first Christmas at Bryniau, and we intended to enjoy it.

With the snow came frost and soon there were skating parties up into the mountains where the pools had frozen over. Skating became such an obsession that even after a vigorous day, the family would set off by moonlight for an extra session, finding their way by the light of storm lanterns.

POD (an affectionate abbreviation for 'Poor old Dad') was always the organizer. One day he came a resounding cropper, leaving a starburst of

cracks in the frozen surface. 'A bang like that does you a power of good. Breaks down the adhesions', was his not very convincing comment.

The skaters were welcomed home with a pan of hot soup or stew. Hot bricks from the oven were wrapped in blankets to keep the beds warm for the tired skaters.

# Food Wasn't Everything

## ARNOLD KELLETT

*Arnold Kellett, a respected local historian and writer, well known for his works in Yorkshire dialect, was in Army Intelligence during the war. Here he contributes a Christmas memory.*

Although Christmas in wartime was boxed in by the blackout and wrapped up with food coupons, it was celebrated much the same way as in peacetime. Indeed, everybody was determined to ensure a few days of comparitive festivity and good cheer as an essential oasis, a well-deserved relief, amidst the gloomy accumulation of war news, air raids, long separations and general restrictions.

Food rationing was the greatest problem, of course. But there were ways round this. Yorkshire housewives, being proverbially thrifty, soon learned how to save up their precious allocation of sugar and other scarce items until they had sufficient for the Christmas baking.

Various economical recipes were devised, such as one for Christmas cake, which included cold tea to give it a darker, richer appearance than it otherwise would have had. Here are the typical wartime ingredients for **Christmas pudding**:

| | |
|---|---|
| 4 oz breadcrumbs | 2 oz prunes |
| 4 oz flour | ½ teaspoonful salt |
| 3 oz suet | ½ teaspoonful bicarbonate of soda |
| 2 oz sugar | 1 grated carrot |
| 1 tablespoonful treacle | 1 grated apple |
| 4 oz raisins | 1 teaspoonful nutmeg |
| 4 oz sultanas | 1 reconstituted dried egg |

Some housewives would manage to enliven the pudding with a little rum or brandy, and others, especially in the country, would include real eggs and butter. The main course at the Christmas dinner was also likely to be better in the country, with a variety of game. Although turkeys had been introduced to Yorkshire in Tudor times, the bird was by no means the standard centre-piece of the Christmas table. Our wartime Christmas dish in the West Riding was usually a chicken or a small joint of pork.

Still, with all the little extras, some of them mysteriously obtained from 'under the counter', and all the warmth of a convivial family get-together, I remember no deprivation during those Christmases of the war.

In any case so much of the atmosphere was quite independent of food and drink. The artificial Christmas trees, baubled and tinselled, came out as usual, along with colourful home-made paper decorations. And, though coal was in short supply, there was always the cosy glow of a real fire – a log fire in the Yorkshire Dales – round which we gathered as we listened to the wireless or played games or sang carols or just chatted in a relaxed and homely way.

It was this gathering round a glowing hearth that I missed most, during my Christmases away from home in the Army. There was no shortage of food and drink overseas, but we missed that vital yuletide ingredient of snow or frost or at least cold weather. The first of these Christmases was spent in the dusty dry heat of Karachi, in what is now Pakistan. I shall never forget one very special compensation there – how the unbelievable brilliance of the starry sky over the Sind Desert brought vividly to mind the journey of the Magi. The second Christmas was spent in the humidity of Malaya – and once again the palm trees framed a wonderful sky, featuring the splendour of the Southern Cross.

The third Christmas was passed on board ship on our way home for demob. The voyage was scheduled to get us back to Blighty in time for

Christmas, but there were various delays, and we sat down to digest an ample Christmas dinner in – of all places – the stormy Bay of Biscay. I don't remember that any of us were actually sick, but our appetite was no longer for food. It was for our homes and families and the girls we'd left behind. We finally landed at Southampton and arrived in York in the small hours at the close of Boxing Day. The Army authorities had provided one of the most lavish Christmas spreads we had ever seen – just to send us on our civilian way rejoicing. I remember how they simply couldn't understand it when – with all the pent up excitement of getting back home after our long oriental exile – none of us could manage to eat a single mouthful.

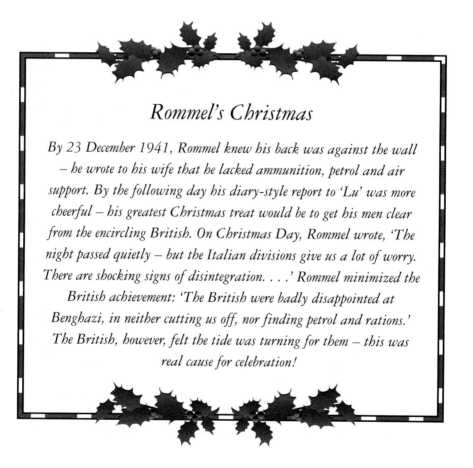

## Rommel's Christmas

*By 23 December 1941, Rommel knew his back was against the wall – he wrote to his wife that he lacked ammunition, petrol and air support. By the following day his diary-style report to 'Lu' was more cheerful – his greatest Christmas treat would be to get his men clear from the encircling British. On Christmas Day, Rommel wrote, 'The night passed quietly – but the Italian divisions give us a lot of worry. There are shocking signs of disintegration. . . .' Rommel minimized the British achievement: 'The British were badly disappointed at Benghazi, in neither cutting us off, nor finding petrol and rations.' The British, however, felt the tide was turning for them – this was real cause for celebration!*

# Iron Rations and Pyramids

*The regiments sent to fight in North Africa and Egypt bring to mind such names as 'Desert Fox', 'El Alamein' and 'Tobruk'. One newspaper report of the time suggested that they 'had it easy' compared with those in other war zones! Here are a few accounts to bring memories back to all the regiments who fought there.*

The men of the 2nd Battalion, Panzer Artillery Regiment 33, were browned off, and not just by the North African sunshine. The pig they had been feeding up into prime condition for their Christmas lunch had been drowned! One of the torrential rainstorms which characterize the winter along the North African coastal strip had caused a flash flood in a wadi and swept the unlucky animal away to its doom without leaving so much as a single slice of bacon behind. All that was left on the menu therefore were the ubiquitous Italian canned sausages.

Rommel was forced to abandon the Gazala Line on 16/17 December and start falling back towards Agedabia and El Ageila. Morale on both sides began to sag as the days to Christmas ticked away, although on the allied side there was excitement during the third week of the month as they approached Benghazi. This was the most important of Rommel's ports (the other being Tripoli) and its recapture could have a significant effect on the campaign.

Unfortunately for the allies, on 19 December – the day they arrived in Derna – an Italian convoy reached the Benghazi wharves and began unloading twenty-two brand new tanks for the 15th Panzer Division, while a similar quantity arrived in Tripoli on the same day. The numbers were small but they were just what Rommel needed to stem the tide of the allied advance.

There was controlled pandemonium in the port as docking facilities were sabotaged, files burned, surviving supplies hurried west and casualties evacuated. Smoke and ashes hung in the damp air, making

the already unpalatable food almost totally inedible as the final Axis troops abandoned Benghazi on Christmas Day. But they left slim pickings for the allied troops who ventured cautiously into the narrow streets. For them it would be canned meat and veg as usual for lunch, for the Germans had already taken the last scrawny chicken which had not found itself in an Arab cook-pot!

Food is one of a soldier's continual preoccupations, alongside sleep, officers, the enemy (on occasion) and that favourite wartime solace, women. And naturally being Christmas, food and drink were among the principal topics of conversation. Unlike other theatres of war, where it was possible to forage in order to supplement the normal ration issue, in the desert it was far more difficult, although the occasional goat would find its way into a stew. The Germans and Italians actually fared worse than the allies, for the canned sausages they received were even more unpalatable than the British meat and veg or bully beef.

These canned meats were supplemented by a daily loaf of bread cooked in the mobile field bakeries, and by tins or pots of margarine and jam and lumps of cheese. Sometimes a food parcel containing cakes or biscuits would arrive from home, but convoy losses were high, and parcels, together with the mail the troops on both sides looked forward to so eagerly, often went to the bottom of the Mediterranean. Many other foods were prohibited, including cold meats and unpeeled fruit, because of the danger of dysentry and typhus from the clouds of flies everywhere.

Tea of course was the main drink on the allied side, brewed over billy cans filled with sand and soaked in petrol which gave a fierce smokeless heat. Brewing up came to have a double meaning in the desert – making tea, or setting an enemy tank on fire.

The Germans had their ersatz (substitute) coffee made out of acorns, while the Italians at least had a plentiful supply of rough wine, which helped make Christmas more enjoyable. In fact, one of the most sensitive issues in the Axis partnership, particularly at this time of year, was the standard of living enjoyed by the Italian officers from monied families, who imported their own luxury goods, while the rank and file had 'dog food'.

Few soldiers on either side had anything like a traditional Christmas. Where did you find a fir tree in the desert? Fortunately there were plenty of candles, a few cartridge cases tossed into the campfire acted as crackers, and for the lucky ones there were presents from home.

A Christmas card sent from Egypt in 1941. (Private collection)

There were church services and carol singing on both sides of the lines – Hitler never succeeded in suppressing Christianity – and the majority of the German soldiers were church-goers, while most of the Italians were of course devout Roman Catholics. Thus soldiers on one side might be able to catch the strains of 'Heilige Nacht' on the air, while their adversaries would hear a squaddie rendering of 'Silent Night'. After church, those off duty could listen to the short wave radio broadcasts of the BBC or the Reichsrundfunk, though the reception was generally poor. There were books, newspapers and magazines to read, and card games or chess and draughts to play. There were letters to be written, and for those who chose a real luxury, some sleep arrears to catch up on.

# Sand and an Old Umbrella Tree

## HARRY 'DON' TURNER

*Harry 'Don' Turner was one of those men who never knew when they had done enough. In the 1920s he volunteered for the Royal Navy, eventually leaving as a Petty Officer. After a spell in Civvy Street in the Depression, he re-enlisted in the Guards, losing any credit for having been an NCO in the Navy. Undaunted, he achieved the rank of sergeant-major, leaving when his time was up in 1938. He re-enlisted at the outbreak of war, joining the Signals Corps as a private. During the Dunkirk evacuation, he suffered a serious blast injury and shell shock, despite which he swam for two miles before he was picked up by the Navy. Instead of being invalided out with honour at that point, he fought to regain his fitness and a front line posting.*

*In 1941 he was assigned to the 8th Army as a dispatch rider, seeing
action until late 1943, when as a result of several illnesses, he found
himself downgraded to non-front line duties. He finished the war as a
physical training instructor with the rank of sergeant, at Catterick.
He died in 1988 having endured bone cancer with the same stoicism that
had marked his service career. Here he describes a Christmas spent in
Egypt, with a rather makeshift Christmas tree.*

I was some distance from the front line that Christmas. The British had
advanced easily against the Italians, before being driven back by
Rommel's Afrika Korps almost into Egypt.

The front line was a bit scattered, or at least the bit nearest me. I
spent most of December 1941 helping to dig vehicles out of the sand,
digging my own bike out, getting soaked by sudden downpours
wearing only khaki drill shorts, and trying to keep the flies out of my
food.

Rations in the desert weren't that good. At HQ in Cairo though, the
officers seemed to be having a good time with plenty of drinks.

Harry Turner, near Cairo,
Christmas 1941. (Private
collection)

On Christmas Day itself, I had to take a message to a forward unit from Cairo. It was some distance into the desert. I got there in the early afternoon, and was given a piece of cold Christmas pudding with some jam on it, while I was waiting for a reply. I remember that the officers and men were all gathered together round the canteen tent. It was quite cold, and I was glad that some heavyweight kit had caught up with me. Some of the chaps were wearing barathea jackets and shorts, while some of the blokes from the armoured car unit looked a bit odd with sheepskin jackets and long shorts.

Everyone was playing whist. There wasn't much else to do. They had tried to decorate for Christmas using strips of fabric and bandages as decorations. There were a few bits of signalling ribbon that had been used as well.

The funniest thing of all was the Christmas tree. Someone had found an old umbrella without any fabric on it, and had half opened it, stuck it in a bucket of sand, and put one straggly piece of tinsel round it! I had some foil saved from tobacco packets which I added to it, and another visitor brought some cotton wool, to make snow on the 'branches'. Whenever someone else arrived they put an extra piece on it. By the time I had to go, it looked very festive.

As each bloke left, a new arrival would take over his cards, so that the game could carry on. I didn't see any money changing hands, but any betting was done with cigarettes or tobacco. One bloke had some oranges that he had 'liberated' to use as a stake, but when he was called away, he threw his remaining oranges to all of us. That was a real bit of Christmas spirit. I think that the oranges were the best Christmas treat of all, because the sand got in everywhere, even into the tea! The oranges had that shiny skin to keep the sand out, they didn't attract flies, and they were very juicy!

I had other wartime Christmases after that, but it wasn't the same back in England with all the rationing. I think those blokes in the desert made Christmas happen for themselves. No one else was going to do it for them!

# Un-Christmassy Headlines

*During the war years, newspaper headlines were distinctly 'un-Christmassy'. People were more interested in what was happening on the fighting front, than what Mr Jones gave his old mother for Christmas. The following reports are from the* Daily Herald *on Christmas Eve 1942.*

*16,400 CAPTIVES TAKEN IN A DAY – Russians push on eighteen miles capture many places.*

Heavy KLIM Voroshilov tanks are leading the pursuit of a beaten enemy who is retreating with all haste in the great Don Bend. Lieutenant-General Filip Ivanovitch Golikov's troops smashed through the German defence walls of ice from the frozen river Don.

*Meanwhile Rommels Army was racing into Tripoli.*

Cairo Radio announced last night 'there is little doubt that the bulk of Rommel's Afrika Korps has reached the Tripoli area'.

*RAF bombers attacked targets in Holland and France on the 23rd, as reported in a story entitled BIG RAIDS ON NAZI BASES.*

Lockhead Venturas, the fast new machines which made their debut in the big daylight raid on the Phillips radio works at Eindhoven on Sunday 6 December, flew out seaward over the Thames estuary at a high altitude leaving vapour trails . . .

Later in the afternoon Boston bombers, also escorted by fighters, bombed the docks at St Malo, Brittany, which the Nazis use as a supply base as well as a port of call for U-boats.

At the same time RAF fighter squadrons carried out sweeps over

Brittany and Normandy to counter possible opposition to the bomber raids . . .

At midnight an Air Ministry communiqué announced that all our bombers and fighters had returned.

*Goebbels was reported to be DOWN IN THE DUMPS.*

Goebbels was in a gloomy mood in his Christmas message, 'Das Reich', yesterday.

'Wherever we look,' he wrote, 'we see mountains of problems which must be mastered. Everywhere the path is steep and dangerous. Nowhere is there a shady spot where we may rest. We must make use of the hour. If it has once gone all possibility of reaching the summit is past.'

*The 'fighting men' of the allies were to send their Christmas messages home in a broadcast.*

At 10.45 p.m. tomorrow, all BBC transmitters will broadcast a half-hour programme in which men of the allied fighting forces from all over the world will send Christmas Day messages of greetings back to their own country.

*And in America:*

A million dollars (£250,000) in war bonds was given away yesterday.

That was the Christmas present of Bernard M. Baruch, adviser on United States economic matters, to war relief and charities.

British war relief gets £25,000. So do Russian and Chinese war relief and the United Seamen's Fund. A sum of £50,000 is his gift to both United States Army and Navy relief.

*CHRISTMAS UNDER THE SWASTIKA – WIVES RISK GESTAPO TO DO THEIR CHRISTMAS SHOPPING is a report from around Europe by Iris Carpenter, on the trial of Christmas shopping under the shadow of the Gestapo.*

British housewives put up with some discomfort – crowded shops and trams and buses, as they do every Christmas, but what about those housewives in occupied countries who are shopping under the eye of the Gestapo? Take an RAF-eye view of Europe's capitals.

BRUSSELS. Madame Louise Renoir is risking imprisonment in a concentration camp to fill her shopping basket – not with presents or luxuries but with enough vegetables to eke out the meagre rationed food.

With hundreds of other housewives she takes a day trip into the country to buy swedes, carrots and potatoes. The guard on the train is a good patriot. Madame Renoir loses no time when he advises her 'Get off this train and catch the next.' So far she has been lucky enough to avoid the Gestapo inspector.

AMSTERDAM. Vrouw Mien Jansen will remember the 'Kerst Krans', that delectable almond-filled pastry of pre-war Christmases. And the tulips that decorated the dinner table. Those tulip bulbs have long since been ground into the bread.

PARIS. Madame Jeanette Dubois can be sure of only one item in satisfactory bulk. That will be bread. Half a pound a day for each member of the family. To get the small piece of meat for the *plat-du-jour* on New Year's Day her family will do with soup and vegetables for the week beforehand.

BELGRADE. There will not be enough bread for Gospodja Milica Yovanovic's family with their ration of under 4 oz a day. And to get that she will stand in a queue in the snow from four in the morning!

PRAGUE. Pani Marie Novokova hopes that she will get a few salt herrings to vary the inevitable soup. And that her meat ration will be in the shops for once if she is there early enough.

OSLO. Only in Norway have the Germans made the smallest attempt to alleviate the suffering they have caused by their ruthless looting of the European larder. Their Christmas gesture of goodwill to the Norwegian housewives is two small tins of sardines and half a pound of minced meat.

# The Fairy Tale of a Mild Winter on the Steppes!

*A Christmas Eve newspaper report recalls the story that the German soldiers were told to expect a mild winter on the Russian steppes!*

TANKS LEAD CHASE ACROSS DON STEPPES – Hitler's commanders are being forced to execute the most massive and the swiftest retreat they have yet made.

The commanding officer of one of the Red Army units which is pressing forward across the middle Don steppe sent this message to mobile headquarters: 'Have captured another fortified village with prisoners, material and German munition and food dumps. No time to count captured stores; my men continue the advance. No enemy ahead.'

Great columns of heavy Voroshilov tanks and medium T36s, having broken through a succession of fortified lines, are thrusting south and south-west through a vast area of open country. Like steel fingers of a searching hand they are driving deep into German-held territory. They are getting so far ahead that they are sometimes even in advance of the sappers who search for minefields. One such tank column reached a river where the enemy had blown up the bridge. In the engineer's absence the crews dismounted under harassing fire and built a makeshift bridge, across which they and the artillery were soon renewing the pursuit.

Between these steel fingers of tank columns, infantry are moving forward, consolidating the captured positions and clearing the country in between, so that solid fronts are soon established. They are tough men these guards divisions now chasing the Nazis. They have been marching and fighting continuously for six days, but they still have a devil of a lot of kick in them.

Their lightning advance is giving them the most astonishing mass captures. Most of these prisoners are a pitiful sight with fingers, feet,

"I'M DREAMING OF A WHITE CHRISTMAS"

Topical Christmas card released after the news of German soldiers being caught out by the weather. (Private collection)

ears and noses frostbitten. They are clad in their autumn uniforms: thin coats, thin short boots wrapped in rags, heads swathed in kerchiefs or dirty towels. They get bitter when they explain their unpreparedness to meet the biting winds and driving snow which they have to face.

'Our officers told us last month', they declare, 'that meteorological experts had come to the conclusion from scientific data, that it was going to be a mild winter, so we were not provided with special warm clothes.'

Enemy losses in the retreat have been enormous. Corporal Dietrich told his captors that his sapper battalion were flung into the line to help the infantry regiment, and the casualties reached up to 70 per cent. In his own company there was not a single officer left.

South-west of Stalingrad the fighting grows fiercer as the Germans renew their efforts to break through to their encircled divisions. Soviet troops, however, continue to repel the Nazi attacks. In some sectors the Germans mustered dozens of tanks and tried to break through by massed blows. Most of the German-held villages have a ring of pillboxes around them, with very heavy fortifications.

# A Right Royal Navy Christmas!

*The lads in the Navy ate well, despite the rolling conditions in which they ate. So said an airman, whose own enforced Christmas dinner on board ship ended up in the briny! Here is a Christmas Day naval menu for 1942.*

Breakfast:      Rolls
Porridge
Mixed grill
Coffee or tea

Dinner:        Tomato soup
Roast turkey and stuffing
Cabbage
Roast potatoes

Christmas pudding and Custard

Tea:           Tinned fruit
and
Christmas cake

Supper:       Murmansk soup
Cold roast pork
Cold ham
Pickles

Mince pies

Not bad eh!

# Christmas Patrol

*The curator of the Royal Naval Museum who provided this poem commented
with an apology that it did not have much Christmas content. In reading it
one is aware that the writer did not have much Christmas content in his
Christmas that year to inspire him to write anything more 'jolly'.*

Never ending, swaying motion,
Deck an inch of oil and ocean,
Bodies thick with dirt and grime,
Mess traps full of grease and slime.
Muscles taughtened, stomachs spewing,
Tossing, pitching, twisting, slewing,
Tempers fraying, limbs so weary,
Eyes so heavy, mind so dreary.

Smell of flesh and food gone rotten.
Filthy plates and meals forgotten.
On watch, off watch, sleeping, waking;
Thought of all things else forsaking.
Laying, huddled close together
On the deck to suit the weather.
Spare torpedoes (may be needed),
Sweat from bulkhead drips unheeded.

Sleeping – not with satisfaction,
Fully clothed in case of action.
Waking with a groan and swearing.
Never change the clothes they're wearing.
Filthy crew space, thick and stinking.
'Precious water' – only drinking.
Rolling, lurching, no resistance,
Dawn till dawn the same existence.

Lighting dimmed – a blackout serving,
Solemn thumping, mind unnerving.
Deck alive with oily mixture,
Nothing seems to be a fixture.
Mess utensils constant rapping,
Steel on iron ever tapping,
Briny dripping, never pausing,
Insane thoughts and movement causing.

Five days out and consolation;
Diving brings a short salvation.
'Neath the surface things are quiet.
Minds and bodies profit by it.
Mental rest, the rolling ceasing,
Aching limbs and muscles easing.
Chance to think, for peaceful resting;
Writing, reading; even jesting.

Short, however, joy and respite,
Short the hours of northern daylight,
With the darkness, bitter raining,
Comes again the hours of straining.
Look-outs lurching, slipping, clinging,
Sleet that's cutting, wind that's stinging,
Spray and snowflakes dancing, teasing,
Straining eyes and bodies freezing.

Then again that swaying motion,
Then again that oil and ocean.
Day by day the same existence,
Day by day with grim persistence,
Searching, seeking, never finding.
Task monotonously grinding.
Drinking water ever draining,
Tinned food, long since all remaining.

At last a recall, spirits rise.
Sweet meditation, shining eyes.
Mem'ries of the past returning,

Now a different aching, yearning.
Mail to greet them? Great sensations.
Thoughts of letters, friends, relations.
'Return to base, patrol is done',
Return to heaven, water, fun.

'Harbour stations', joy is mounting,
Minutes now, not days they're counting;
For a time their task is over.
Bathed and cleaned they'll be in clover.
'Stepping off' to mix with others.
Writing mail to sweethearts, mothers.
Men; with hearts and feelings blended.
'Uneventful patrol' ended.

# Dreadful Stories

*Wartime humour had a certain 'earthy' feel to it: everyone was familiar
with the double entendre. Here are two festive examples.*

## All Part of the Service

The Women's Voluntary Service were giving a Christmas party in 1942 for
a newly-arrived group of Poles, who, having endured captivity at Russian
hands, were about to embark upon a lengthy course of flying training.

Many of these Poles had only a sketchy grasp of English. One of
them, quite awestruck by the appearance of so many worthy matrons in
uniform, ventured to try out this strange language. Selecting what he
believed to be the most important lady in the room, he coughed.

'Excuse please beautiful lady, what is uniform?'

The grand lady (large, white-haired, certainly over sixty years old), replied in very portentous and ringing tones, 'This is the uniform of the Women's Voluntary Service!'

The young Polish airman looked both impressed and dumbfounded. Slowly light dawned in his eyes. 'Ah! In Poland we have to pay!'

# A Shocking Exposure

Picture the scene: the morning of Christmas Eve 1943, in darkest Lincolnshire. The weather was foggy, raw, and distinctly unfestive. Three airmen doomed to pass their Christmas at a far-flung dispersal, were ministering to their Lancaster bomber. They were exiled from the cheery lights of the sergeants' mess, let alone Mum's home cooking. All of them were feeling somewhat miserable, faced with spam, stale bread, and not much in the way of warmth in their Nissen hut.

Realizing that they would not be missed, the three heroes set out on a foraging spree, hoping to commandeer anything that would add to some festive spirit.

Cycling into one quiet village at lunch-time, they happened upon a goose grazing upon the common. With one accord they fell upon the unfortunate bird, hoping to stifle it before it drew attention to its impending appointment with their Christmas menu.

Rapidly they stuffed the (by now) apparently inert bird, down inside the ill-fitting battledress of the smallest airman, buttoning it in before the village bobby appeared.

Well pleased with their efforts, they propped their bikes against the wall of a nearby hostelry, and repaired to the public bar, which was deserted save for a buxom young barmaid and a rather large, bullish landlord.

Seeing the airmen served with three pints of bitter and some salt biscuits, the landlord went into the saloon bar, only to be summoned back by a dreadful piercing shriek. He ran into the public bar, only to see a couple of biscuits on the counter, three half-empty pints, no airmen, and the barmaid in a dead faint on the floor.

'Elsie, love, what happened?'

He patted her into consciousness. Terrified, the girl looked up and

blurted, 'Oh it was awful . . . awful . . .' With a choking sob, she lapsed back into oblivion.

'Blimey, this means brandy!'

Gently, he coaxed some of the burning amber liquid between her pallid lips. Slowly, colour returned to her face, and once more her eyes opened.

'Oh it was awful, I can't say, it was awful . . .'

''Ere Elsie, come on, I can't afford any more brandy.'

'It was terrible, I've never seen anything like it!'

'Now, now Elsie, it was those airmen wasn't it? I thought they were up to no good. Come on girl don't faint again!'

'Yes, yes, it was 'orrible!'

'You're a big girl now Elsie, you've seen that sort of thing before! One of them exposed himself didn't he?'

The barmaid sobbed, convulsed with shock at the memory of this dire event.

'Yes I have, but nothing like this! I've never seen one before that lifted itself up, and took a biscuit off the counter!'

That takes the biscuit! Cartoon by Giles Thomas. (Copyright Giles Thomas, 1995)

# I Remember a Wartime Christmas . . .

*The following short memories have been gathered over the years from war veterans and their families. Their memories take us from the manger in Bethlehem to a prisoner of war in Leeds, and from a pre-war Budapest to a Franciscan convent by a Hindu temple in India, and wartime Christmas through the eyes of children. Of all our calendar festivals, Christmas has survived pretty well intact in its main principles of 'peace on earth, goodwill to all men'; acknowledgement to God; thoughts of family; and extending the 'milk of human kindness' to those on the 'other side' - even in the harsh reality of a wartime Christmas.*

## War in the Frosty Air

### MARJORIE CARTER, SOUTHAMPTON

In December 1938 I was in Budapest giving English lessons to Jewish families who were hoping to leave Hungary if Hitler's armies should ever cross the frontier. My Scottish friend Dorothea, married to Mihály, a Hungarian, had asked me to spend Christmas with them in the little town of Harvan.

I arrived on Christmas Eve to a sumptuous meal of wine soup, turkey and various sweetmeats. Mihály, Dorothea, an aunt and uncle and a young lady cousin sat around the table. A tall tree stood in the corner of the room bedecked with presents and tinsel. Micky, aged four, and Agnes, aged two, were delighted with some red leather boots. After the children were in bed we all unwrapped our presents with much excitement.

Later some of us walked to Midnight Mass through soft rain gradually turning to snow. On our return we drank Tokály (a delicious wine) while listening to records, until tired out we went to our beds.

I awoke at nearly midday. The world was white under blue skies. After coffee and rolls, Dorothea tucked the children in the horse-drawn sleigh, bundled in various parcels, then we climbed aboard and with a jingle of bells sped through the crisp air, stopping en route to deliver and exchange gifts and heartfelt greetings to their many friends.

Back at Dorothea's house a group of gypsies were invited in to sing carols, accompanied by their lilting violins, as we ate our lunch.

All too soon I was sitting in the train to Budapest dreaming of my white Christmas – and wondering if it would ever be the same again. There was something in the air, an unease, a restlessness. What was to come? Would we meet again in Christmas 1939, or would the fates change the path. . . .

# Late 1930s to the War

## MRS BATTERSBY, NEWPORT, GWENT

When I was young in the 1930s, poverty abounded, yet my wonderful Mum always managed to give us a good Christmas and would bring family and grandparents home on Christmas Day. In the afternoon the children entertained the adults with their cabaret which they had been rehearsing for weeks.

It was only at Christmas that we had chicken for dinner. Sometimes Mum would make a change and have duck instead. In the weeks prior to Christmas she would spend many hours pickling red cabbage and making her puddings.

By the time the 1940s came, the family gathering began to dwindle because members of the family were joining up or being called up for the forces. There was rationing and a scarcity of many things. I remember carol singing with my two close friends; we would go round the houses with our little song book. We never knocked on the doors but just sang our carols. We usually had a response. My childhood Christmases were happy times and there was an abundance of warmth and love in the home; that is something money can't buy.

# The Big Red Bus

ALAN WILLEY, NEWPORT, GWENT

The first Christmas I remember was 1939. Dad went to the market in Dock Street where they sold off the meat cheaply at the end of the day. On Christmas morning I had a big red bus that lit up, with switches all over it!

I also remember when my grandfather kept a fruit and veg shop (James Cahalane) in Maesglas. My brother Terry and I used to go to the shop on Boxing Day where he loaded us up with all sorts of nuts and oranges for our trip to the pantomime at the old Empire Theatre. The drummer there had the biggest drum I had ever seen, and I, being at the 'little horror' stage, proceeded to bomb it with my ammunition of nuts!

In 1952 I was in the Army. Just before Christmas I got the news I was going to Korea; I came home on embarkation leave during which my nineteenth birthday fell due. Mam and Dad laid on a combined birthday and Christmas party for me. I swear I never saw so many people in a semi-detached house before or since!

Two weeks later I was on my way. We stopped in Japan for a few weeks, and I just had time to send a few gifts home. Then I was sent to Korea. As I came off duty on Christmas Eve, the sergeant gave us the marvellous news that parcels had arrived for us. I opened mine to find the most beautiful cake, and several other things. I learnt much later it cost a fortune to send it. Then I realized what wonderful parents I had.

# Christmas Twins – for a Moment

JOHANNE EAVES, LONDON

Christmas morning, 1940, I got up just to go to the toilet. I thought my husband was annoyed, thinking I had got up to make early tea. He had intended to get our first Christmas morning tea – during the time we had been married I had made morning tea.

At this time I was pregnant, expecting our first child in February 1941. I was longer out of bed than it takes to make tea, and my

husband came to investigate. By this time I had realized something unexpected was happening.

My husband dressed quickly and rushed out to phone the hospital for an ambulance. Sure enough labour pains had started and by 11 a.m. I was the proud mother of twin girls – the hospital's first Christmas twins.

I felt so privileged and excited. Alas, my joy was short lived; my babies were small and weak, and conditions in those war days were not as good as they are today. My babies were put into intensive care; I was asked if I would like to have them baptized and I said 'Yes'. That afternoon the priest – the hospital padre – left his Christmas lunch to come and baptize my babies. A Catholic nurse who had attended me was their godmother.

My babies were kept in intensive care; I did not see them again. In those days mothers were kept in bed for about eight days after giving birth.

On 29 December, my first-born died, on 2 January the second one joined her sister. They shared Our Lord's birthday, and in a short while they shared His kingdom too.

I have often thought of and prayed for that padre; I'm sure my two 'special saints' do too.

# Poles, Piles and Aussie Pilots

### F.D. KELLY, KENT

Christmas 1942, I heard Midnight Mass in a cave packed with Poles, in an Army hospital at Mosul, Iraq. 454 Squadron, Royal Australia Air Force were intended for the first line in India, when the Nazis penetrated the Caucasus; the snow-tipped mountains we could see to the north. But they never did!

I had haemorrhoids, dysentry, desert sores and sprue (a killer tropical disease). The hospital, a casualty clearing station, consisted of caves blasted into a cliff, fresh air being supplied down shafts by fans. The Poles who had travelled south, while we moved north, took over the hospital from the Indian and British armies. They suffered terribly to reach Mosul. In the skin ward were cases of scabies, tetanus, seborrhoea,

impetigo – described by the British MO as the worst he'd seen caused solely by dirt.

A Polish custom was to toss our burly RAMC corporal three times to hit the ceiling while chanting cheerily. Corp., a caring man, was reduced to tears!

The matron offered a prize for the best decorated ward, ours being judged the 'most cheerful', but every ward got a prize! The medical ward was the most artistic, because a commercial artist from 454 was sent in by the CO when he heard about the prize (to win it for our squadron), to join the jaundice cases from 454, causing the ward to be nicknamed 'Canary Corner'.

'To a Polish soldier, Wie Zyjo Polska. Greetings from New Zealand. The Polish Army League', is on a gift card I received and still cherish. Food was sparse, as supplies were short. An ancient gramophone churned out 'Old Shep', a Bing Crosby number about a sheep dog.

It was a truly memorable Christmas, which I shared with those heroes, the stout-hearted Poles.

# A Palestine Christmas

### D.J. TURNER

At 7 p.m. on Christmas Eve 1942, I was on a so-called local Arab form of transport (to call the contraption a bus would be sacrilegious!). My pal, who was Church of England, was with me, and about thirty of us set out for our destination: Bethlehem.

As we chugged along at a steady 20 m.p.h., and took the hairpin bends of the Seven Sisters with such cries of alarm from our Arab driver, cursing sheep as we rounded each bend, it was a relief to be finally greeted by a guide at exactly 11.55 p.m. outside the most beautiful church I have ever seen.

People of all nations were milling about, seeking entrance for Midnight Mass. We were directed to the main entrance and as Mass had begun, a priest beckoned us to follow him. To the side and rear of the church, steps led down to small tombs each with about twenty people standing in the enclosures. I ended up in the tomb of St Jerome! Gerry my pal was filled with awe. It was a wonderful start to Christmas.

# No Room at the Inn

JIM TREACY

In 1942 I was serving with the armed forces in Tel Aviv. On Christmas Eve I went to the bus station to make my way to Bethlehem via Jerusalem. There it was chaotic and almost impossible to get transport. However, the authorities provided a special bus for servicemen and eventually I reached Jerusalem.

I made my way to the Catholic Women's League Hostel inside the old city walls only to find it full up, and the two buses they had ordered for Bethlehem already fully booked. It was hopeless trying to find a taxi, and there was no alternative but to wait and hope I could get on one of the buses. My patience was rewarded and soon I arrived at Bethlehem.

Nothing seemed to have changed since that wonderful night nearly two thousand years ago. It was a bright, moonlit, starry night – the shepherds' fields clearly visible below. Thousands of people of all nationalities were milling around, many trying to force their way into the Church of the Nativity.

There was certainly no room in the inn and it was easy to visualize Mary and Joseph, somewhere in that crowd, looking for shelter for the royal birth.

A church close by the Church of the Nativity had been reserved for Midnight Mass for the troops. This was an unbelievable experience, but for me the night had not yet finished. A priest whom I had known in England, asked me to be server for his Mass. What a privilege to serve in a church so close to the spot where Jesus was born.

Every year since then, at Midnight Mass, my thoughts go back to that wonderful night – an event which is engraved forever in my memory.

# Heilige Nacht – Bethlehem 1942

HERR DOKTOR 'HEINI'

I was an internee at the beginning of the war. My work in the Holy Land before the war left me vulnerable once those areas were occupied. As a doctor I had certain privileges, and I was able to do something for

the men who were injured; the atrocities of the war on both sides left me weary of soul. I had managed to get to Bethlehem in the early hours of Christmas Eve, mainly by bribery! Though I cannot say my bribery bought me much comfort – the carts, asses and finally bus that I travelled on left me saddle- and everywhere else sore for days to follow! I had travelled on the outside of the overcrowded bus, hanging on for dear life, and falling off once on a precipitous bend! Fortunately for me some of the packages strapped to the roof also fell off, so the bus stopped to pick them up – I think they would not have afforded me that courtesy!

I arrived at the Church of the Nativity in Bethlehem at around 0700 hours. I had been advised by my captain, who had visited the church in better times, that I should go there immediately and find a place because it would quickly fill to capacity, and I would not get in. I found my way to a group of small enclosures – the chancery chapels I suppose, of various saints. Here I stayed; I ate a piece of stale bread, a little Italian sausage and drank from my bottle. This was to break my fast of the previous eleven hours, and begin my fast for the next twenty! There was activity all the day. Visiting priests of all nationalities were saying Mass at the different points of the great church. While it was still early enough, I risked leaving my gear at the tomb, and walked around the church. I visited and touched the silver star set in the floor where the traditional place of the manger was. I attended a Mass being said by an Italian Army chaplain – the familiar Latin wafting over me like a soothing balm.

I did not dare to go towards the great main doors to look outside, or buy any souvenirs from the vendors there, for fear of losing my place. It was a milling throng of people coming and going, and by now, at nearly midday, mostly coming. But I did manage to send a small boy on an errand for me. He was begging, with crutches. I had been warned that there were many such, and often the crutches were fake. But this child turned blank milky eyes to me – here was no fake. In spite of his deformity, he seemed capable of finding his way around, so I asked him to get me some souvenirs for my family, and also indicated that I was hungry – mostly by sign language! Giving him money, when he did not return in the hour, I began to have doubts, but there he came, using his crutch most effectively to make room for his path I thought, and smiling a wide cheerful smile, which wrenched my heart. Here we were, Christian men, fighting, maiming, killing for power and greed – and

here this small boy showed us all up for what we were. He had nothing, yet all he asked was a chance to show that he was useful and trusted.

His selection of trinkets were not what I would have chosen, but they were as precious as gold to me. So was the huge fresh loaf and hunk of cheese, which stank to high heaven, but *was* heaven to me! At least I would have something to eat after my vigil was over, for I was determined to observe a Christmas vigil. I needed the spiritual healing of this pilgrimage, and meant to do it properly.

Returning to my tomb, I settled down with my prayer book – given to me by my mother; it was my constant solace. I think I may have slept a while, because I was suddenly aware that the church was heaving with people, and a choir was beginning to chant. My tomb was suddenly filled with British soldiers. I was afraid, I should not be here! But the Mass had begun, and no one took any special notice of me, until one of their group, a camp padre, began to hear confessions of the men. I spoke English well enough at that time even, and went forward to this representative of the one God we all shared. He gave me the familiar Latin blessing and I poured out my soul. Later the padre gave out Holy Communion. I had not presumed to join the British men then, but he came to me, and several of the men patted me on the back and shoulders. I wept.

After the war I came to England where I finally made my home. It was some years before I was able to find my family and send them the trinkets I had bought that Christmas Eve in Bethlehem. They were all safe, thank God, unlike many who perished, and later we were re-united. But I was never to see my parents again.

# I Sang in the Choir at Bethlehem

TOM LENNOX, SUNDERLAND

The most memorable Christmas in the sixty-eight I have known is that of 1942, when I found myself present at Midnight Mass in the Church of the Nativity at Bethlehem.

As a humble private soldier I felt overawed, not only at being present, but at being part of the choir, whose hymns were to be broadcast to the world. The sense of awe experienced in no way

inhibited the joy at being there, on the anniversary and at the very place where Our Lord was born.

The sense of anticipation as we waited for Mass seemed to make it easy to pray; your thoughts turned to your loved ones and though they were so far away, it now seemed that they were close to you. One thought of Midnight Mass in your own parish church, shared with your family and friends; the return to your house where Mother presided over cutting the first slices of Christmas cake, allowing the younger ones to share in a glass of rhubarb or elderberry wine. The lovely feeling experienced as the family sat and talked around the big coal fire.

I remembered the Christmas Mass of the previous year, 1941, when we stood amid the rubble of the remains of the Catholic church at Tobruk, only the altar and some wall was standing. After Mass when the priest spoke to us, I noticed battle-hardened soldiers losing the fight to restrain their tears as they thought of home, especially those who had children.

Two weeks before Christmas 1942, I found myself in hospital in Jerusalem; there I served Mass for the chaplain. The priest was very patient over my Latin responses but then he knew I was a Geordie; he probably thought that as it was difficult for me to speak the King's English, so my attempts at Latin were to be tolerated. *Mea culpa*!

On Christmas Eve the chaplain told us he had permission to take some of us to Midnight Mass; what excitement as we climbed into the back of an Army truck, and the chaplain announced that we were to be in the choir. Many times along the road, he took us through our parts – the Kyrie; the Gloria; the Credo, etc., until we considered ourselves equal to the Treorchy of Wales! Alas, I cannot remember the name of the chaplain who enabled me to have this wonderful Christmas memory but I have thanked him every year since.

The hospital in Jerusalem was said to have been a German palace built either for or by the Kaiser, in the days when Palestine was in the Turkish Empire.

I remember where the priest said Mass; it was a sort of large alcove just inside the main staircase. The stained glass was magnificent as was the view which overlooked the city.

The hospital was on either Mount Scorpus or the Mount of Olives, I now forget which. I wonder if there is anyone left who travelled in the back of the Army truck from Jerusalem to Bethlehem that Christmas Eve, 1942?

# A Place called Timimi

JOHN CARDEN, LIVERPOOL

By late 1942, the Battle of El Alamein was over and the opposing forces were in retreat. We as a tank regiment having been in action all the time, were 'pulled out' at a spot in the desert called Timimi. Christmas Eve arrived and a chaplain arranged for Midnight Mass to be celebrated at a map reference equidistant to all regiments in the brigade; I travelled with the chaplain as a server.

The altar was the tailboard of a 15 cwt. truck; no altar cloth, no lit candles (the Luftwaffe were very active). The night was clear and bright as only a desert night can be, the stars hung so low and the sky as a backcloth was deep blue – a typical desert night.

From all points in the compass men appeared. Our chaplain gave general absolution and he then celebrated a simple low Mass in Latin. One man had a mouth organ and we sang carols during Mass as we knelt in the sand around the makeshift altar. The fervour and faith of that congregation could be felt. There were about sixty of us, all had travelled some distance on foot.

When Mass was over, we wished each other a happy Christmas, then went our separate ways, all thinking of loved ones so far away, and feeling – in a sense – united by this occasion. Since then I have attended many Midnight Masses, but that simple Mass in the desert is my most enduring memory.

# Italian POWs at Dereham

MARY JORDAN, BOGNOR REGIS

It was wartime, 1943, and our first Christmas Eve spent in the pleasant little Norfolk town of East Dereham, where my husband was stationed in the RAF. The church we attended was a very modest affair with a tin roof, so Midnight Mass was celebrated in a large room in the town hall.

Just before it began came the sound of heavy boots, and in were marched the Italian prisoners of war, with armed guards in attendance.

Canteen at King's Cross underground station shelter, Christmas 1944. (London
Transport Museum)

The Mass was in Latin, which must have been a comfort to them, and,
at the end, the priest most kindly read from a paper a few words of
greeting in Italian for them. Then they were marched out.

On Christmas Day the weather was cold and snow had fallen. On our
old bikes we cycled along the flat Norfolk fields. Several times we saw
little groups of prisoners, huddled together against the cold. We waved
and called out a greeting, thinking of our own dear soldiers in such
cases, and hoping someone was doing the same for them.

Our Christmas dinner was a luxury – a chicken from a local farmer,
too big for our tiny oven, so we had to tie the door with string! For
dessert, two cakes from the local Salvation Army.

In spite of the uncertainties, pending postings and separation, that
Christmas held a peace and confidence that I have never forgotten.

This is a story of the last Christmas I spent with my in-laws in
Cheltenham. My boy was then at Sandhurst. At Christmas 1943, he

came home to Wembley Park, having special leave that he did not know he was getting, so I had arranged to go to my brother-in-law for Christmas as my husband was with his brother on sick leave from the airforce, being a reserve from the First World War. He was called up after the Battle of Britain.

However, I telephoned Cheltenham and said I would not be coming as my son had just arrived home unexpectedly. Fred said to bring him up too, and his girlfriend, so we all went!

It was a wonderful Christmas – such food and laughter from Fred who was manager for a store like Harrods.

Fred could do fifty impressions and was a second Charlie Chaplin! We all went to Midnight Mass and slept like tops when we came home after having a double whisky each.

Christmas Day was great, with all the presents under the tree. Dennis my son, and Betty his girl, went for a long walk on Boxing Day as we were leaving late. Dennis had to be back at Sandhurst and Betty and I at our offices, the next day. My husband, being on sick leave, should not have travelled with us but he decided to do so. As all of the family came to see us off from the station, my husband was walking in front with his brother and his young boy. Dennis said to me, 'Slowly Mother, and do not turn your head.'

Two red caps had stopped Francis, and my son walked up to them. They stood to attention and saluted him, including his father. Whatever he said to them, they let hubby go with another salute!

When we all got into a carriage we had a laugh, as the red caps could not see his white ribbons on his shoulder underneath his British greatcoat, so did not know he was an uncommissioned student officer! He went back to Sandhurst and was commissioned on 4 January, his twenty-first birthday. Those dear boys had to learn six years training in five and a half months.

He could not have the regiment he chose because he had not the £800 year private income, but he was given the next best crack regiment, the Fife and Forfar Yeomanry.

He was posted to Bridlington, and each time he brought down a regiment to King's Cross, he would telephone my office at Somerset House and say 'Mrs L', and my boss would come to me and say 'King's Cross'. I used to fly and get a cab to meet him, and if he could not squeeze me into his jeep, I'd go on to Victoria and wait under the clock until he arrived. I had several of these calls, and always went to meet

him. I did not know the last time, when we said goodbye and he held me close and kissed me again and again, that he had been planning and preparing for D-Day in the South. He was only twenty-one when he was killed in Caen, and was buried in Bayeux. From college to Sandhurst and his grave was only eighteen months.

# POW Carols at Romsey

### MARY BRYSON, CARDIGAN

During the bleak years of the war, when there was an atmosphere of despondency and gloom, my widowed mother and I had an invitation to spend Christmas with a farming family, where my younger sister was posted in the Land Army.

We lived in Ealing where we had the strain of constant air raids, never knowing whether we would be alive from one day to the next. In addition to this we had the deprivation of food rationing and the queues for bread and other essentials – in fact my Saturdays were spent outside a shop in anticipation of a delivery of oranges or some other scarce commodity.

This change from the dreary town scene with the blackout at night and shortages of everything, including fuel to keep us warm, came as a wonderful tonic. The log fire was burning in the grate and my sister was able to join us in the living room after she had helped with the milking – done by hand then. The farmer's wife and four children were Catholics so the highlight of our visit was Midnight Mass in the chapel at Romsey Abbey.

It was snowing when we arrived, but there was a welcome that I have never experienced since. The crib and chapel had been decorated by Italian prisoners of war, who were also singing the carols. The whole atmosphere was one of joy, warmth and peace among men. We were all one at that Mass, Catholics and non-Catholics, and nationality alike. One could feel the faith and hope and love generated.

The journey back with the moon shining on the snow-laden trees was of breath-taking beauty and we were alone down that winding country lane but our thoughts were still with the Christ-child and his peace. Somehow just the memory of this 'other world' helped me to survive the 'doodle-bugs', V-II rockets, and even further shortages with the ending of the Lend-Lease at the end of the war.

Candles, choirboys and carols for Christmas – come what may. Midnight
service at Winchester, Christmas 1940. (Private collection)

# From the Diary of a Cameron Highlander

## P. MCERLAIN, MIDLOTHIAN

PANCHIGANI, INDIA, CHRISTMAS 1943 – Moved out of jungle after three long months of jungle training. Camped under canvas outside this little Indian town, garrisoned by the Rajpitani Rifles. Three days later it was Christmas Eve and we turned out in force for Midnight Mass. Our RC padre and the good nuns were delighted at our turn-out and we crowded into the little church looked after by the nuns. There in that beautiful church ablaze with candles and masses of flowers around a pure white marble altar, we forgot about the hardships we had been through.

We listened to the pure clear voices of the nuns' choir, and seemed to be in a different world. Another time, another place, that uplifted the soul and gave us a glimpse of heaven that we had forgotten about. I looked along the rows of tough, sun-tanned comrades and wondered if their thoughts were the same as mine. Many of them never heard another Midnight Mass, falling by the wayside in action; including our beloved padre.

Somehow it did not make sense, as here we were celebrating the birth of the Prince of Peace and at the same time being trained to kill and be paid for it. However, the padre soon made it clear in his sermon.

'Young soldier, whither goest thou? You who have come from a far country to soldier in this strange and mysterious land.'

'I go to fight against an evil aggressor who has enslaved millions of people. I go to set them free.'

Somehow this sermon gave the war a new meaning and became more of a crusade. Our padre died that grey morning we attacked – and many others with him. Through many dangers, toils and fears we heard his voice again and again: 'Set the people free!'

# This is your Lucky Day!

## CECILIA DE LACY, CO. FERMANAGH

On 23 December 1943 a telephone call announced, 'This is your lucky

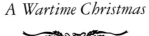

day'. Imagine my joy when I heard the news of my soldier husband's safe arrival in England. He had been away for two and a half years in the Middle East and as a prisoner of war in Germany and Italy. Now I heard he had escaped from the prison camp and after eleven weeks on the run had arrived at British lines, and eventually England and home.

My baby daughter Anne was two years and three months old and had yet to see her daddy for the first time. In joyous haste I decorated the house for a very special Christmas after three lonely years. I prepared a special meal – not easy in wartime England. I dressed my baby in her best fur-trimmed coat and bonnet. However, the excitement wore her out and she was fast asleep when, at last, the doorbell rang!

What a wonderful reunion. This had to be the best Christmas ever! We shared our joy with relations and friends, and shared too, our carefully hoarded delicacies.

At my husband's request we invited two German POWs stationed nearby to share our beautiful day. After a celebratory Christmas dinner, we all gathered at the local church for carols and blessing. We were filled with happiness and gratitude for my husband's safe return. As the strains of 'Silent Night' filled the church, tears streamed down the faces of the prisoners of war, remembering no doubt their loved ones far away in Germany.

To us all this was a Christmas never to be forgotten.

# Christmas in the Vatican

### E. HENNESSEY, LEEDS

In 1944 I was in Italy with the RAF and was fortunate to get leave to attend Midnight Mass in St Peter's in Rome. Though common enough now, that year was the first year in history that a Pope celebrated the Christmas Mass publicly, so this was memorable for more than one reason.

I was uncertain about the procedure, but when I went into the college which was run by the Catholic Women's League for the forces, there I met an old school friend, Father Mills, a Jesuit and RAF chaplain. He put me in the British allied Choir, and our place was at the side of the altar. From 10 p.m. motets were sung by the Sistine

Choir, and carols sung by the allied forces in their own languages, and the final carol was 'Silent Night', sung by the Swiss Guard in German.

At 11.45 p.m., Pope Pius XII entered the basilica to the sound of silver trumpets playing a triumphal march. Finally the Pope appeared carried aloft on the papal chair; the crowd cheered, and there were shouts of, 'Viva il Papa!'

He arrived at the central altar under the magnificent Bernini bronze canopy and celebrated a low Mass. At the end of the first Mass he distributed Holy Communion to hundreds assembled near the altar. Among the group were German and Japanese ambassadorial staff and diplomats of the allied forces.

According to the ancient custom dating back to times when a priest had to travel around to different areas, and needed to celebrate more than one Mass on Christmas Day, the Pope celebrated a second Mass, after which he resumed his seat, and the procession returned the full length of the basilica, led by the Swiss Guard with red plumes in their hats. Then followed the dignitories and prelates of the papal court, and finally the Pope, held aloft so that everyone could see as he gave his blessing to the crowds. Tears were in the eyes of everyone thinking of their loved ones at home.

This has to be *the* most memorable of wartime Christmases – an historical 'first' occasion, but more special than that was the sight of the allies, with the Germans, Japanese and Italians all together to celebrate the birth of the Prince of Peace. A few short months later the war ended. Maybe it was the combined prayers of everyone present praying, as they assuredly must have been for an end to this massacre, and a beginning of peace on earth and goodwill to *all* men.

# Midnight Mass on Stand-by Alert

M. CANNON, BRENTWOOD

In December 1944 I was stationed with my tank regiment in Holland. To the south of us the Battle of Ardennes was raging and the German advance was endeavouring to cut off the British and Canadian armies. Consequently, the division of which my regiment was part, was on a stand-by alert.

On Christmas Eve I had obtained permission to attend Midnight Mass at a nearby convent, part of which was military headquarters. I was the only Catholic in my troop and permission was given provided I was fully prepared to join my crew in an emergency. So, encased in my tank suit, with my side-arm strapped on, I trudged through the snow to the convent.

At the convent chapel I found, amongst the Dutch congregation, a number of British soldiers all carrying arms like myself. Before Mass began, the whole congregation led by the clergy and nuns rose and proceeded to the small hospital attached to the convent, prayed in the ward with the patients, and then returned to the chapel where Mass began.

On leaving the chapel, every single soldier was stopped by a nun and directed to a small hall. To all our amazements it was set out with decorated tables with immaculate tablecloths, sparkling cutlery and laden with food and fruit that must have taken all the rations of the convent.

We sat down in a kind of stupor, and then the Mother Superior addressed us in perfect English.

'Gentlemen,' she said, 'at this time you will be thinking of your homes and loved ones. We nuns hope that for a short time we can bring them closer to you by providing a little of the comforts of home.'

Can you imagine the effect upon us sitting at those tables, waited upon by nuns? An oasis of peace and sanity in a world gone mad.

As I walked back to my unit in the snow, I thought of that night nearly two thousand years ago, with a greater peace than I have ever known.

# Carols in Shepherds' Field, Bethlehem

### J.L. HORNBY, LEEDS

At Christmas 1944, I was in Jerusalem on seven days' leave. At that time I was staying with Toc H, and on Saturday 23rd was lucky enough to obtain a ticket for Midnight Mass on Christmas Eve, at the Church of the Nativity, Bethlehem.

A party of us set off by bus that evening, passing Rachel's Tomb before reaching Bethlehem, about five miles south of Jerusalem. On arriving we walked down to Shepherds' Field, where, with many other nationalities we sang carols before a huge bonfire. The night was very cold and it was not hard to imagine a night similar to this two thousand years before. We then proceeded up towards the church in silent groups, as if by talking we would break the spell of this magic night.

We found the church packed to the doors. It was just before midnight, and I, with a group of others, was led down to the Crypt of St Jerome. We stood there, for the last few minutes to midnight, the priest then started the Mass, and each of us received Holy Communion. I cannot conceive any other time in my life to surpass that one.

# A Franciscan Christmas in India

### J.D. WILLIS, LONDON

During the war I was stationed for a while in Trichinopoly in south India and for several years I returned there from other parts of India to spend Christmas with an Anglo-Indian family who had befriended me. One of the most memorable amongst many Christmases abroad was that of 1944.

As is the custom, we spent the early evening on 24 December, decorating the house and after an early meal we prepared for Midnight Mass. About two miles outside Trichinopoly was the island of Sri Rangam, which was formed by a bifurcation of the great Cauvery river. On this island stands an ancient Hindu temple of great size and fame, also a small ashram inhabited by some six or seven Franciscan friars. It was their small chapel that we had decided to go to for Mass on Christmas Eve. We went in a small covered tonga pulled by a pony and set off into the Indian night which was quiet, warm and still; I remember the stars were spread about the sky in their thousands.

We made our way to the small monastery which was a collection of thatched huts. There were some fifteen or more local parishioners and we set off around the small island in a procession, singing carols. I

doubt if the Adeste Fideles ('O come all ye Faithful') ever sound more appropriate. On returning to the small chapel into which we all fitted with some difficulty, the crib was blessed and the few friars sang Mass. Never had plainsong sounded to me more beautiful. The poverty and simplicity of the whole place was so fitting and so in keeping with that first Christmas.

As the years have sped past I have never forgotten Sri Rangam, and each Christmas my thoughts return there.

# Guess Who's Coming to Christmas Dinner?

### LUCY TERESA ALADICS, LEEDS

Just after the last war I was accompanying my father on a Christmas morning visit to his family, when we passed a German prisoner of war sauntering towards the city centre. He was boldly identifiable by the black cross on the back of his greatcoat.

'What a rotten Christmas Day for this poor fellow!' murmured my father.

As we returned home, we passed him again. 'Do you think your mother would mind if we asked him home for Christmas dinner?' asked my father.

'I'm sure she wouldn't,' I said, and excitedly hurried on ahead to prepare my mother for our unexpected guest.

My father approached him in German, and brought him home, protesting that he would not come in unless my mother welcomed him, which she generously did. He had previously experienced hostility from people on his few excursions from the camp.

He was a most courteous and gentle man, a Lutheran minister in his own land. He spoke some English, and with my father's own knowledge of German we were able to communicate.

He would have left immediately after the meal, saying that he did not wish to spoil our Christmas, but he was persuaded to spend the whole day with us. How amazed we three young sisters were to find that the 'enemy' was no different from ourselves.

.g months before his repatriation, he became a
parents sent parcels to his wife in Germany. I
.ed cod-liver oil capsules!
.ed with my father, but his letters became increasingly
.out life in East Berlin. Eventually they ceased altogether,
.easure the silver fish slice which he sent us as a token of his

# Camels and Kings and Jingle Bells

M.C. RUSSELL, BLACKPOOL

I have a wonderful, happy memory of Christmas 1945, just after the
war, as a nurse in a small children's hospital in north London.

Several little ones had been bombed out of their homes; some were
crippled with arthritis.

Each member of staff did a display of a carol. I was allocated the hall
and stairway areas. I did the 'Three Kings', making camels and kings
and drawings of the city of Jerusalem up the stairs, and 'Away in a
Manger' in a huge fireplace in the hall itself.

Each child wrote a letter to Father Christmas and everyone received
whatever they had asked for – even to a silver bracelet! I was given the
privilege of going to a large factory to receive a beautiful, good-sized
tree, fully decorated, which arrived a few days later, and was set up and
further decorated with presents.

At midnight I kept watch while Matron went round leaving
stockings and presents on each bed. The joy of those little children the
next morning was wonderful to see. In the afternoon, Father Christmas
came round the grounds on his sledge with presents for each one, jingle
bells ringing. Happiness filled that little hospital in spite of the pain or
illness of those children – thanks mainly to a very dear and good friend
in the Matron.

One of the 'reassuring signs that life goes on even when lights go off',
Christmas advert, 1939. (Private collection)

*from*

# Thank You Padre

## JOAN CLIFFORD

*In this extract from her book of wartime reminiscences of the many services padres, Joan Clifford, a clergy widow, gives a wonderful insight into that unsung group of servicemen.*

All padres made utmost efforts to celebrate the great Christian festivals and this was usually appreciated by the troops. Diaries and memoirs stress the importance of Christmas, though the ambivalent nature of this celebration has to be acknowledged. For many serving troops, with little Christian background, it was a holiday and they would get the most from it. There was inevitably a lot of drunkenness as the day wore on. Bill Story, who travelled round scattered camps on his motor bike, was saddened when a Hindu officer commented to him, 'What is this Christmas? I thought it was a religious festival.' Bill says, 'Of course, he had not seen into any of the churches – only what went on in the streets and the canteens.'

The chaplains went to great lengths to see that the men had a good time, with extra rations and cigarettes, but also did their best to draw them to early services.

The musically talented John King, in Laufen POW camp, produced a service of nine lessons and carols, in all details following the pattern of the service he had loved at King's College, Cambridge. This involved arranging the service totally from memory and scoring the music, since they possessed no printed scores. Amazingly, a full orchestra was gathered together from camp residents, with instruments provided by the Red Cross. The Germans, with their reverence for good music, and the knowledge that large numbers of inmates would be for a time safely and harmlessly occupied, facilitated the provision of the instruments. John King was delighted with the result and so was everyone else. After affecting this in the Laufen camp, King repeated it,

under much less promising conditions, in his Polish camp at Schildberg. 'A wonderful day,' he wrote, 'in spite of everything. I think this is one of the very best evangelistic services. The sweep of the lessons is quite majestic.'

In a small camp on the outskirts of Munich run by a Scottish sergeant-major, Raymond Bowers went to conduct a Christmas service. He wanted the entire camp to be present, and the sergeant-major declared it would have to be held outside, for lack of space. So they cleared an area and piled the snow high all round. 'It was bitterly cold,' remembers Bowers, 'and I kept everything brief – a couple of carols, short prayers and readings, and an address and a blessing. When we hurried back to the hut and were thawing out, I asked the sergeant-major if everything had gone off all right. "Aye," he said, "but I thought, sir, the sermon was a wee bitty short. . . ."'

The ship *Penelope*'s assignment was the protection of British supply ships to Malta, and she escorted several convoys and survived several dive-bombing attacks. Christmas 1941 was approached by her captain and crew with apprehension. Would there be raids? But all was well, as reported by her chaplain, John Inderwick-Palmer. 'We were able to start our midnight Communion service to the accompaniment on the bosun's pipe of "Raiders Past", the next best thing to angels singing, "Peace on Earth, Goodwill toward Men". . . .'

# Polar Bears for Christmas

## R.A. RASEY

*'Ras' as everyone knew him, was a Met. Office character. With his sleeveless jumpers, rolled up shirtsleeves and engagingly wicked grin he was a man who could smell Gatwick's all too pervasive fog, and didn't care very much for going along with a consensus view when it came to forecasting. If he believed that the weather was going to be hazardous for flying, he would stick to his guns in the face of opposition from other senior forecasters, with whom he had to agree the 'story' for London's three airports every day. During the war, Ras was posted to that graveyard for Atlantic depressions, Iceland. The job was vital but unlike today's non-stop flights from Los Angeles to London, guided by computer and electronic highways, speeds were slower, aircraft range and reliability was far less, aircrew were inexperienced, there were no navigational aids, and weather forecasting was an art. The following account is a distillation of many notes made in the late 1960s when Ras was coming to the end of a very interesting and varied career.*

The war pitchforked you into responsibility whether you wanted it or not. It hadn't seemed all that long ago since I was in training school learning about saturated adiabatic lapse rates and so on. I remember there was one lad on my course who wrote that cirrus clouds were composed of 'blocks of ice!' I think the upper wind must have been very strong to keep those up there!

Iceland was a funny posting. When I look back on it, it always seemed to be winter. Even in south-east Iceland you're not far from the Arctic Circle, so daylight was almost non-existent around Christmas time.

You needed a lot of cooperation from everyone taking observations at sea, in the air, and on the ground, in order to draw up a chart. International cooperation was good, except of course from the Germans

who had other ideas. Usually these observations weren't broadcast by radio for any great distance. Aircraft would come back to their bases with observations on cloud, air temperature, etc. and if the navigator was really good at taking drift sights, or calculating true position by astro-navigation he would be able to tell you the wind speeds.

Sometimes this information was several hours old. Some boats would take the risk of radio broadcasts of information, but this was very dangerous, as German U-boats would home in on these signals.

Most of all, we relied on poor devils who were stuck in some God-forsaken hole, battered by winds, taking half-hourly observations all through the day and night. In addition to recording the surface weather, they often had to send up hydrogen balloons which they tracked with a theodolite and stopwatch in order to assess the winds aloft. In December that was very difficult, as the light was always bad, and the cloudbase was sometimes on the deck.

North-western Iceland was the most remote area. Although the pack ice didn't really reach that far south, icebergs did. These icebergs would drift across from Greenland, and there were many stories of polar bears and seals coming across with them, although I never saw one.

I remember we had one young American sailor who was being dispatched out to one remote out-station in the north-east before the winter really set in. He was going to have a very lonely Christmas, seeing no one else for about twelve weeks. His only link would be a teleprinter back to Keflavik.

A great deal of effort was put in by the signalmen to make sure that the line was kept open. I told him: 'If you feel a tap on your back . . . run!' He asked why, so I told him that the area was uninhabited and that it would most likely be a polar bear! He was most upset, as polar bears had a reputation for biting first and asking questions afterwards.

There was always a risk of the Germans landing a raiding party from a submarine to put these remote stations out of action. It took a great deal of bravery, and self control to man these stations for three months at a time. Imagine spending Christmas with no other human contact.

What did happen at Christmas though has become a Met. Office tradition. Operators, having sent their observations back, often would compose ditties, or patterns with letters, and transmit them back as Christmas greetings. You would find Christmas trees or crib scenes sent down the wire made up entirely of Xs or Is. I suppose doing this kept the men sane.

*from*

# Winter in the Morning

## JANINA BAUMAN

*In 1943 the Jewish family of Janina Bauman, her mother and her aunt, escaped from the Jewish ghetto to the 'Aryan' side of Warsaw where they had a room in a farmhouse in a quiet village, owned by Christian Poles (the Pietrzyks). Drawn into a different world, where they were expected to attend church with the other Christians to avoid suspicion, it was a difficult time. The following extracts are from Janina's teenage diaries, describing Christmas preparations in the host family's household.*

**19 December** – Great excitement in the cottage: preparations for Christmas have been going on since last Friday. First they stuck a pig – in great secrecy, of course; it should have been handed over to the Germans. Then everyone in the family worked hard to make the pig meat into joints, lard and sausages. Once they had finished with the sausages, they started whitewashing the walls. It was our turn yesterday. Blazek appeared with his bucket and brush and we moved into the kitchen. We sat there cosily as it was snowing like mad outside, and helped Mrs Pietrzyk peel vegetables, sort peas, grind poppyseeds with sugar, and mend Blazek's old trousers. The old woman first sang canticles in her rusty voice, then started telling us stories about her family. She had had eight children altogether, and had outlived three of them, as well as her two husbands.

Her eldest daughter lives with her own family somewhere far away, the other one has given herself to God and lives locked away in a convent. That's why Piotr, one of her younger children will inherit the farm. Blazek is not fit to be on his own she said, he is far too daft . . .

Three days before Christmas Eve, Blazek brought two fragrant fir trees from the nearest wood. To our surprise, one of them was for us. We somehow managed to tuck the prickly thing into the gap between the bed and the window, and truly embarrassed, wondered what to

hang on it. But Mrs Pietrzyk had worked out the whole matter in advance. Soon she appeared with a roll of bright coloured paper, two pairs of scissors and a jar of flour and water paste: 'It's for you, ladies. Show us what you clever townsfolk can do!'

We set about cutting up and sticking the colourful strips with true zeal. It was sweet to sit in the warm light of the kerosene lamp, breathe in the fresh scent of the tree and produce the rustling chains and fluffy balls. It brought back memories of childhood to all of us.

Within a couple of days all the decorations were ready except for the most important one to go at the top of the tree. Our burst of creativity suddenly deserted us and we couldn't think what would be best and easy enough for us to make. At last I decided to try and make a star. Since I had never been good with my fingers, I took great pains with it. There was no gold or silver paper, so I had to use blue. When I had finished we all put the stuff away since, according to Polish custom, the tree should be dressed by dusk on Christmas Eve.

We felt very uneasy about the approaching festivities, fearing we might do something wrong and show our ignorance of Christian traditions. To make it worse, two ladies from Warsaw who had befriended Auntie Maria in the queue for free meals, insisted on spending Christmas Eve with her, but claimed that the place they lived was not good enough for the occasion. Auntie Maria could hardly say no, which meant they would come, meet the rest of us and be able to watch us closely for hours. We really dreaded it.

On the morning of the crucial day, we dressed our fragrant tree, and very pleased with ourselves since it looked gorgeous, called Mrs Pietrzyk in to let her see it and marvel at it. The old woman scanned the tree, nodding with approval, then stepped back and glanced at the top with special attention. Her expression changed, her jaw dropped, she clearly did not like what she saw. Taken aback I followed her gaze to the top of the tree, and shuddered: in full daylight, against the background of the whitewashed wall stood a six-pointed blue Star of David, the emblem of the Jews.

Mrs Pietrzyk said nothing and left, but after a while she came back with a gold cardboard angel of impressive size. 'This would look better, if you ask me,' she said flatly.

Christmas Eve which we had dreaded so much, turned out rather well. The two Warsaw women arrived in festive mood and seemed very friendly. One of them, a dressmaker, had lost her husband in the war; the other, a chiropodist, was a spinster. We had an almost traditional

supper, since Mrs Pietrzyk presented us with borsch and noodles with poppyseed, and the ladies also brought some food to share. Before we began, all the Pietrzyk family came in for a while to break the wafers with us. Then we sang carols and really enjoyed ourselves; despite our earlier misgivings everything worked out fine.

Since they mixed with other people far more than we did, our two visitors knew quite a lot about what was happening far away from the quiet village. The Red Army was still waiting idly in the Warsaw suburbs across the Vistula, but rumour had it that the Russians had steadily advanced everywhere else, pushing back the Germans with breath-taking speed. At the same time, the Nazis were losing in western Europe and the Third Reich was clearly approaching its bitter end. The final victory of the allies was now close.

As we parted from our visitors, the dressmaker warmly embraced Mother and said, 'Hope for the best my dear. You've endured the worst. God will help you till the end.'

'It won't be long now,' chimed in the chiropodist.

They had guessed our secret.

*from*

# The Woodpecker Story

## VIVIAN JACOBS

*Despite the horrendous assaults on mind and body endured by our fighting forces, many still managed to put on the traditional pantomime. Stories endure of sailors manning their guns dressed as good fairies and dames during alerts coming in the middle of their festive entertainment. In 1943, an RAF Squadron (136 'Woodpecker') in the Arakan, were planning to make it a good Christmas – complete with a pantomime. Here is an account of the event by Squadron Leader Vivian Jacobs.*

With but a few days to go before Christmas, Johnny Rudling and Pete Kennedy grabbed their scripts and threw themselves into a wild rush of rehearsing. On his days off and at nights, Pete could be heard singing lustily from a hilltop where he had taken himself off to learn his lines in solitude, whilst Johnny was often observed making endearing remarks to a piece of soap while squatting in his little canvas bath, his script propped up on the grass beside him. On Christmas Eve the dress rehearsal was held, and as dress rehearsals go, it went.

Next night, Christmas night, after a day of readiness when it was sure the Japanese would strike, but didn't, there was the traditional Christmas dinner when officers and NCOs waited on the airmen. The family was all together at last, lacking only a small group still in Calcutta, including, unfortunately, Don Chapman, who had been involved in the conception of the panto, but who was hard at work in Calcutta putting the Christmas edition of the *Oasis* to bed . . .

Everything was in readiness for the panto – then came a scramble which resulted in the 'star', Johnny Rudling, being badly shot up, landing safely but with a Japanese bullet in his Mae West collar, a small matter which concerned him less than the fact that he was due on stage any minute! Well 'dosed' with the necessary (for shock treatment of course!), he appeared on cue. However, his 'medication' had a dire effect on his performance as the plot unfolded. . . .

After a rousing overture by the Arakan Symphony Orchestra (three pieces of it anyway), a line of seven 'oriental' gentlemen presented themselves front stage, wearing coolie hats, and to the background of 'Strike up the Band' from the ASO came the opening chorus:

> As the curtains part and our show we start,
> Don't expect a scene set in China.
> For although we know this Aladdin show
> Is Chinese we thought India finer!
> Ere you start to depart at the sound of that name,
> We would say, please do stay , it's OK.
> And that you soon will find it's no bind,
> Pantomime's all the same – see it through!
> So here we go! On with the show!
> The Woodpeckers present . . . Aladdin!

At which the oriental gentlemen nodded their heads to disclose letters which spelt out the title of the show.

As the curtains parted – no hitches yet – to reveal a bevy of dainty Bengali belles, the roars of laughter that greeted their appearance set the tenor for the reception of the show all the way through. There were mistakes aplenty which only added to the enjoyment by the audience; had they been planned they could scarcely have been bettered. The stage manager hadn't seen the show before so was definitely playing it by ear . . .

Then there was the fervour of the ballet. Petunia, the ugly sister – Dougie Chard – lost her tiara at the height of her endeavours to escape the clutching hands of the Wicked Uncle – who was no mean clutcher – and Gloria (the 'beautiful one') tripped daintily across the stage, gradually gathering speed, to launch herself into the arms of Aladdin, only to have the pair of them collapse in a heap centre stage.

There were many high spots. Nothing so mundane as a magic lamp; this Aladdin, because of his mother Widow Twanky's proclivity to char, had a Genie of the Teapot, who got around on a scooter! The Sultan of Shambazaar (a slightly insalubrious suburb of Calcutta) had a need of 'Auntie Maggie's Remed-ee!'. He was a bit of a lecher on the side, and in his turban were strategically placed red and green navigation lights, which lit up and flashed with a passion when their owner saw something of which he liked the look – to whit, Widow Twanky! But the magic cave contained the rarest object in all India, jewels beyond price – Spitfire tyres!

The ballet, as all good ballets in musicals should, helped tell the story of the piece and move the plot along. In this case there was Gorgeous Gloria (heavily veiled, as was Petunia) longing for Aladdin and the Wicked Uncle who had eyes only for Gloria, but was impeded by the interfering attentions of Petunia, poor soul. Meanwhile Aladdin was delayed elsewhere, discovering this fantastic hoard of Spittie tyres.

As the quiet opening bars of the second side (old fashioned 78 r.p.m.) of Ponchiella's 'Dance of the Hours' began, or were supposed to begin, a glamorous ballerina entered daintily stage right and beckoned to a friend stage left. They posed prettily then realized the music hadn't started; what they thought they heard was probably a lonely elephant calling to his mate, out in the jungle somewhere. Exit both ballerinas in confusion. In the wings they exacted a promise from the record player, saw the needle dropped gently into place, made sure they heard the first notes and cantered rapidly into place. The piece proceeded through its gentle exploratory and story-telling paces of the

The ballet with Johnny Rudling as Aladdin, centre. (Squadron Leader Vivian Jacobs)

quiet movement then suddenly hurled itself, along with the dancers, into a frenzy of activity of whirling arms, legs, flying bodies, heaps upon the floor, to the triumphant conclusion with Gloria in Aladdin's arms (or it might have been the other way round, as Aladdin was having some difficulty standing – due to the shock of finding all those tyres). The Wicked Uncle reached out hopelessly for Gloria while being firmly clutched by Petunia. As the curtain drew down on that little number, everyone was paralytic with laughter.

But Uncle was not to be so readily put off, having succeeded, by his evil powers, in gaining possession of the magic teapot. He was about to 'have his way' with Gorgeous Gloria, when who should arrive on the scene to scotch his plans, but the brave, daring, handsome, Aladdin, mounted on the front seat of a jeep, one foot planted heroically on the bonnet. Now there hadn't been time to rehearse the MT driver; he had just been told to drive Johnny on to the stage and stop. But Aladdin at that moment was rushing to rescue Gloria from a fate worse than death

at the hands of the Wicked Uncle and, seeing his beloved in those evil clutches, he shouted with some urgency, and happily, coherence, 'Stop, Stop!' which the MT did with alacrity, resulting in Aladdin sailing as gracefully as a Woodpecker over the bonnet of the jeep and arriving in a gibbering heap at the Wicked Uncle's feet. Resultant hoots of laughter verged on pandemonium on both sides of the footlights.

Calm having been restored, and the plot of the play pretty well sorted out, with everyone getting his/her just desserts, the four principals: Aladdin, Gloria, Wicked Uncle and Petunia moved forward for the curtains to close as they went into the Quartette from Rigoletto. The audience didn't know that they were going to mime the recording. Well, the artistes waited for the curtain to close, the curtains waited for the music to start, and the music waited for the artistes to move forward, who were waiting for the curtains to close, etc.

Hoarse stage whispers from all four performers to play the *** records, pull the !!! curtains or put out the *!!? lights brought roars from the audience and startling results from the stage-hands – the lights went out, the curtains pulled and the record started; but it was the wrong one!

Almost without exception, the 'female' members of the ballet had offers to walk home that night, but each replied in varying degrees of basso profundo butch voices that they would take a taxi! The CO gave permission for a celebration party. A fair tribute to Johnny and Pete the Ace and to all the airmen who had put so much effort into giving the rest of the squadron a fine capper to their Christmas festivities.

# Reuters' New Year Report

## ARTHUR OAKESHOTT

*Arthur Oakeshott was Reuters' special correspondent with the home fleet.
Faced with all the hardships of front line service, these correspondents were
rarely recognized for the service they gave, reporting back first hand
accounts at sometimes fatal costs to their own safety. Fortunately, Arthur
did survive, and as a small tribute to him, and all his fellow wartime
correspondents, we print this small report of a New Year's Eve attack from
the* Daily Telegraph, 9 January 1943.

A BRITISH NORTHERN NAVAL BASE. Friday. The Captain of the
flagship of the British Naval forces escorting the the convoy gave me
his own account of the action:

'On New Year's Eve,' he said, 'I saw gun flashes somewhere east of
Bear Island. The admiral's decision was, "Let us march toward the
sound of the guns." We did. We put on 5,000 more horsepower than
we were authorized to raise.

'At 9.40 a.m., the destroyer escort signalled: "We are being
attacked." We had a lot of reports until finally we sighted two objects
which were obviously bigger than destroyers. We opened fire at
11.28 a.m. and hit a ship, very much larger than a destroyer, at 14,000
yards. So did our accompanying ship. We were closing in like hell.
During the next five or ten minutes, the range went down to 9,000
yards and struck the enemy force amidships. The enemy's shooting was
good – but ours was better.

'He turned to the east, but we closed with him, as we did not want
him to get back to the convoy. As we too turned east, we saw an enemy
destroyer 6,000 yards away. We opened up and hit it with the first
salvo, and asked the admiral for permission to ram it. He gave it, but

before we reached it the enemy vessel was in a terrible state, and we passed astern leaving it to sink with the bows well in the air.

'Later we sighted two of the bigger enemy units and opened fire at 14,000. One was hit. Then our ships came under very severe fire from the two bigger units. We were peppered but sustained no casualties. Shells dropped near us and holes were made in the admiral's cabin.

'By this time it was 1 p.m. and we could not see the fall of shots. At the height of the 'party' a young navigating officer, in pauses between gunfire, took a shot at a collection of stars and within a few minutes with his sextant had arrived at the precise position where the ship was situated. Up to five salvos hit the enemy ship, and our accompanying ship confirmed the figure five.

'It was a very successful party. Whatever the name of the damaged enemy cruiser, it sustained very heavy damage and will be out of commission for a very long time.'

That was the verdict among the men who fought her.

Much of what took place will remain a secret, probably until the end of the war, but I can say that behind this clash in the cold and bitter waters of the north, lies a story of naval courage, bluff and daring seldom equalled in any other war.

# Something Awful Every Night: Stories of ENSA

*At thousands of camps in England and France, the routine of military life, the impending danger like a huge cloud over one every moment, and the boredom of waiting for something to happen would have laid low the*

*morale of tens of thousands of service men and women if they had not developed the capacity to enjoy home-made entertainment, especially so at Christmas time, when they could not get home to loved ones.*

*To a large extent the problem was to get the troops to entertain themselves, to find the talent latent in every unit and use it. At the same time, the professional entertainment of the British Army was being well looked after. Basil Dean, who was organizing war entertainments on his own initiative in the First World War, formed ENSA (Entertainments National Service Association), a voluntary organization comprising most of the brains and talent of show business.*

*ENSA was officially recognized on 8 September 1939 and a fortnight later sent out twelve concert parties to entertain at camps all over England. Since then nearly one hundred shows were given every night somewhere in England and France. The entertainment provided included variety, straight plays, dance bands, films and pantomimes.*

*Enough equipment, sets and lighting equipment were carried by these travelling troops to give a performance anywhere, even on the roadside.*

Hitler may not have been popular – but taking a rise certainly was! An ENSA concert 'somewhere in Britain', Christmas 1939. (Christmas Archives)

*The whole organization was centralized in Drury Lane: sets, administration, groups rehearsing, etc. But even so ENSA could not amuse everybody all the time. So the brunt of the job of entertaining still fell to the amateurs; to the unknown and undiscovered comedians, singers and musicians in khaki.*

# A Christmas Champion

*All through the war Gracie Fields worked tirelessly, attending concerts, broadcasts, charity fêtes. A cutting from a wartime paper gave tribute.*

When announcing their Christmas broadcasts, the BBC would say to the press, 'All the stars – including Gracie'. The one and only Miss Fields would be heard; without her no programme at such a time would seem complete.

Gracie Fields singing at one of the field concerts during the war. (Private collection)

During the war this artist had two labels bestowed on her. 'Greatest democratizing agency in Britain', announced the Americans, and, 'Britain's Number One War Industry', a Lord Haw-Haw aside. The Troops epitomize those two comments, when she shows up at one of their camp concerts – she is simply 'The Greatest Number One!'

# Major Glenn Miller is Missing

### GEOFFREY BUTCHER

*No wartime sound was more evocative than that of the Glenn Miller Band, broadcasting across the world to American servicemen everywhere. Couples met to his music in the local palais, troops relaxed to the strains of his music on the field. His was* the sound of the forties, and in particular *of wartime. The following is an account of his disappearance from the book* Next to a Letter from Home, *published by Mainstream, the story of Glenn Miller and his all-soldier band which he created in 1943 and brought to Britain after D-Day.*

It was still freezing cold on the 21st and again Haynes and Dudley drove to SHAEF [Supreme Headquarters Allied Expeditionary Forces] to confer with General Barker and Major May. Still they had heard nothing of Major Miller or his companions or even of any wreckage, and the General said it boiled down to three possibilities: they might have strayed over enemy territory and been shot down or taken prisoner, crashed in a remote place and not yet been found, or gone down in the Channel. Sympathetic as he was, General Barker said that the casualty report *must* be released next morning and promised that he and Major May would see them at the Palais de Glace concert that evening.

When the news of Glenn Miller's disappearance reached the BBC it was more than a personal shock to those who knew him and worked with him. It presented them with what Maurice Gorham later described as the programmes' 'worst crisis'. There were several reasons for this. First, the BBC was broadcasting the pre-recorded programmes by the Allied Expeditionary Forces Band which were all announced by Major Glenn Miller, and as his disappearance had not yet been publicly

announced by SHAEF it would have to continue broadcasting these programmes until SHAEF announced he was missing. After the SHAEF announcement it would still have to broadcast the pre-recorded programmes as scheduled but would have first to remove his voice from the recordings. But it would need to know exactly when to do this otherwise it might reveal that he was missing before SHAEF announced it officially. And of course, he might still turn up. But looking beyond the immediate future, the BBC had to face the possibility that if Major Miller did not turn up, the band might be sent back to the USA or disbanded, and so leave the AEF programme without one of its three house bands (the one with the largest broadcasting schedule of the three) and nearly four hours a week in the programme schedules to be filled in some other way.

Second and of more pressing concern, was the forthcoming Christmas Day broadcast 'The AEF Christmas Show', due to include a live contribution from the AEF Band for which the BBC had at last obtained the use of the only land line from Paris to London. The line was still under the control of the US Army Signals Corps who were operating it for the SHAEF and who were extremely unwilling to allow the BBC to use it at all at that time.

The US Army finally agreed to the BBC having access to the line on Christmas Day for three specified periods only: 2200 to 0100 hours on 24/25 December for Midnight Mass, 1330 to 1500 hours for a contribution to the BBC's annual round the world 'hook-up', and 1800 to 2000 hours for relaying the AEF Band from the Olympia Theatre. Now that the promise of the land line had ensured that the AEF Band's broadcast could go ahead, it had been publicized in advance, but Major Miller's disappearance might mean that the AEF Band would not take part after all. It also presented the BBC and particularly producer AC2 Ronnie Waldman, who was in charge of the AEF Christmas Show and would be compéring the London end of it, with a more technical problem. Besides the AEF Band relaying from Paris, the British and Canadian bands would be taking part in the show from the Queensbury Club in London, and the complicated cues and switching instructions already worked out between London, Paris, New York and Toronto would probably have to be revised in the light of Miller's disappearance – but strict military security prevented any alterations being notified to the other countries before he was publicly announced as 'missing'. And there were only a few days to go before the broadcast!

A copy of the 8th Air Force casualty list arrived at SHAEF on Friday 22nd, where by now it was common knowledge that Major Miller was missing. Formal confirmation of the news was sent at once to the headquarters of the US Army in the ETO [European Theater of Operations] with a request that an immediate radio casualty report on Major Glenn Miller be sent to the War Department in Washington and suggesting that in view of the forthcoming Christmas Day broadcast and the publicity already given to it in the United States, the news be released to the press at 1800 hours (ETO time) on 24 December, making sure that Mrs Miller was informed first.

At 6 p.m. (London time) on Sunday 24 December, the press release was given to the newspapers and radio organizations. It read: 'Major Alton Glenn Miller, director of the famous United States Army Air Forces Band which had been playing in Paris, is reported missing while on a flight from England to Paris. The plane in which he was a passenger left England on 15 December and no trace of it has been found since its take-off. Major Miller, one of the outstanding orchestra leaders in the United States, lived at Tenafly, New Jersey, where his wife presently resides. No members of Major Miller's band were with him on the missing flight.'

# The AEF Christmas Show

GEOFFREY BUTCHER

*After the report that Major Glenn Miller was missing had been released, the BBC – despite earlier anxieties that they would lose the show – broadcast the AEF Christmas Show, made even more poignant now that Glenn Miller was gone.*

The BBC's AEF programme was interrupted just after 6 p.m. on Christmas Eve 1944, with a news flash announcing Major Miller's disappearance. It was also included in the 9 o'clock news on the Home Service. 'Major Glenn Miller, the well-known American band leader is reported missing; he left England by air for Paris nine days ago. Major Glenn Miller came over from the States earlier this year to direct the American Band of the AEF, which has often been heard playing in the Allied Expeditionary Forces programme for the BBC.'

The band resumed its schedule on Christmas Eve with a concert at the Olympia Theatre in the afternoon and another in the evening.

Christmas Day was a busy day. Early in the morning the entire unit attended a special Mass for Major Glenn Miller at the Madeleine church in the centre of Paris, arranged two days earlier by Morton Downey. After Mass the band had a 10 a.m. rehearsal at the Olympia Theatre, an afternoon concert and a radio recording, and another concert in the Olympia Theatre in the evening, part of which was the special live Christmas broadcast.

Over that Christmas period some of the regular programmes in the AEF programme were dropped to make way for special Christmas features and Christmas editions of some of the best shows such as Command Performance. But the high spot for many listeners on Christmas Day was the AEF Christmas Show from 6 p.m. to 8 p.m., devoted entirely to all three bands of the AEF – the only time they all broadcast together in the same programme.

The first half hour went to the Canadian band, the second the British band (conducted by its leader Sergeant Eric Robinson as RSM Melachrino was away on Christmas leave), the third to the American band, conducted by Jerry Gray and compèred by Paul Dudley, and the last half hour was a 'combined round-up' of all three bands, ending with the American band playing, 'Oranges and Lemons'. The Canadian and British bands' contributions also included popular guest stars, among them Cyril Fletcher, Gwen Catley and Teddy Brown and, as planned, the second hour was also broadcast to British listeners to the Home Service. The Canadian and American bands were relayed by short wave to Canada and the USA and broadcast live. The American band's part in the programme was the first live music programme broadcast from Paris since the fall of France in 1940. Producer and compère, Ronnie Waldman, linked the whole show together on the air and after the trials and tribulations of the previous few days the entire broadcast went like clockwork.

The London end of the broadcast came from the Queensbury All Services Club where the British and Canadian bands played to a packed audience of servicemen and women. Manager John Harding later recalled an unexpected incident that evening, 'When . . . the dramatic message was received at the club that Major Glenn Miller was reported missing on a flight to Paris, I witnessed the most spontaneous tribute in my forty years' experience. Unrehearsed and unasked, three thousand

uniformed men and women stood up together in silent sympathy for the loss of one who did so much to provide entertainment when and where it was so badly needed.'

The final 'grand round-up' of the AEF Christmas Show was given a recorded repeat in the 'Morning After' spot in the AEF programme on Boxing Day, and recorded extracts from the show were broadcast in the General Forces programme on Thursday afternoon, 28 December.

Throughout the last week of December the regular programmes by all the Miller units were broadcast from London as usual in the AEF programme, using the pre-recordings made in Bedford, except that on Boxing Day the Tuesday evening programme of the full AEF Band was replaced by a gala production entitled 'Ali Sadsack and the Forty Quartermasters – an unbelievable pantomime for the AEF', with an all-star cast of AEF programme regulars. The Friday evening broadcast of the AEF Band was a recording made on 25 November with Major Miller's voice replaced by an announcer.

By 29 December a welcome transformation had suddenly taken place in the availability of the Paris to London land line. After all the difficulties the BBC had encountered in getting the line for the Christmas Day broadcasts, Gorham was told that the AEF programme could have the use of the lines from Paris at any time of any day without the danger of interruption by military authorities during a programme. The Christmas Day programme by the AEF Band had shown that the sound quality of the transmissions was good enough for all AEF programme purposes, both live broadcasts and recordings, including music. . . .

Although Major Miller was lost, his objective was not. Even without him, the band was able to carry on as he would have wanted, bringing to the troops 'a hunk of home'. It was to continue its work for another seven months, until the AEF called it back to America in July 1945.

# Not a Dry Eye in the House

ERIC TAYLOR

*In Eric Taylor's book* Showbiz goes to War, *there is a description of the inhabitants of Charlottesville, Virginia, flocking to see a war film, made by the Ministry of Information, entitled* Christmas under Fire. *In this*

# A Wartime Christmas

*chapter is what must be best described as a 'soliloquy'; a narrative over the film by the American* TIME *magazine war correspondent, Quentin Reynolds. In subtle movie technique and imagery he made a subliminal plea to the United States for help. The following starts just before his narrative begins.*

His voice replaces the noise and crackle of the burning city, as the camera switches to the platform of a London underground station, where people huddle close together, and then on to a small Christmas tree by the side of which, three or four very young children are sleeping. As a quiet background to his low voice, a choir is singing 'In Excelsis Deo'. He begins:

'It's not a very large Christmas tree. There's no demand in England for large trees this year. They would not fit into the shelters or into the basements and cellars with their low ceilings. This year England celebrates Christmas underground . . . The nation has made a resolve, that war or no war, the children of England will not be cheated out of the one day they look forward to all year. So, as far as possible, this will be an old fashioned Christmas in England, at least for the children.'

Reynolds went on to tell of the serious business of survival that the adults were involved in, protecting their families in that year of the blitz when the German Luftwaffe dropped their lethal cargo of bombs over London.

As he is speaking, calmly presenting the facts, the film shows vivid contrasting images of Christmas decorations, sprigs of holly over an entrance to a garden shelter, paper streamers dangling from the empty shell of a terraced house in London's East End dockland and of guns and barbed wire. But the most vivid and moving of all these images are those of small children in a nursery school. This provides Reynolds with a link between Britain and his American audiences, when he goes on to say:

'Christmas here this year will not be the same as Christmas that children in America will be lucky enough to enjoy. England is fighting for her life and even the smallest child understands that.'

If the smallest child knows that Britain is fighting for freedom against the evil might of Nazi Germany, then the implication is that surely adults must see that too.

In the closing stages of the film when the choir of King's College, Cambridge, are singing 'Adeste Fideles' (O Come, All Ye Faithful), Quentin Reynolds concludes:

Children sleeping under the tree in an underground shelter, 1940. (Private collection)

'There is no reason for America to feel sorry for England this Christmas. England does not feel sorry for herself. Destiny gave her the torch of liberty to hold, and she has not dropped it. She has not allowed the stormy waves of terrorism, which are sweeping over the world from Berlin, to let that bright light even flicker. She is thankful that when the test came she had the high courage to meet it. And today England stands, unbeaten, unconquered, unafraid. On Christmas Eve England does what she has done for a thousand years: she worships the Prince of Peace.'

As soon as Reynolds has finished speaking, the sound of the choir and organ takes over and the camera pans across the platform of the underground tube station shelter picking out significant images: mothers and fathers carefully opening out blankets and covering their children, a mother is holding a baby in her arms, the baby's innocent-looking face is peaceful and lovable, then there is a long shot of the whole platform, showing people settling down for the night.

Slowly then, with the choir now singing softly, the film comes to its close. There is not a dry eye in the house.

Finally as the audience in Charlottesville's Paramount cinema pocket their handkerchiefs, the youngest chorister's unbroken voice soars aloft with the Christmas message: 'O Come, All Ye Faithful'.

Were Americans going to stand by and do nothing? Were they going to walk on the other side of the street while a bully stood over a bruised and weakened opponent? The film does not directly ask that question. But it was there in the minds of all who left the cinema after the show.

The film had used highly evocative music and emphasis upon children, religion, and the sentimentality of Christmas to make a direct appeal to the American people to support British mothers and fathers protecting their children.

What is also remarkable in the film is the subtle way that the words and images are linked to the American way of life as if to emphasize the fact that this war was not one that just concerned Europe, but America too. For example, when Quentin Reynolds said that, 'Destiny had given Britain the torch of liberty to hold' the words immediately conjured up the image of the Statue of Liberty and how in every American's mind it stood for the greatest single symbol of American democracy.

Films such as *Christmas Under Fire* and its forerunner, *England Can Take It*, a ten-minute picture of life in London during the day and night raids of the Battle of Britain, made by the Ministry of

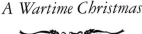

Information, were soon making their impact felt all over the United States.

But that was not surprising for it was part of an overall plan which Prime Minister Winston Churchill had set up. It was in 1940, when Britain was in that life-and-death struggle with Nazi Germany, that the beleaguered British Prime Minister called upon the film industry for help.

With all her allies defeated, Britain stood alone in facing the might of the German war machine that had smashed its way across Poland, Holland, Belgium and France to build up a reputation of being an unstoppable juggernaut. American help was urgently needed.

# Pantomime Time – ENSA or No!

### ERIC TAYLOR

*The entertainment, and thereby morale boosting, of the troops was as important as any military campaign, and the stars endured the same conditions as the fighting men they entertained. Forces sweethearts like Vera Lynn and Anne Shelton would endure bitterly cold venues and hard driving conditions, sleeping rough under mosquito nets. One account tells of Bing Crosby crooning away to a guest audience of fellow stars such as Fred and Adele Astaire, Jack Buchanan, Anthony Eden (then Foreign Secretary) and other worthy notables, while doodle-bugs flew overhead. The famous Windmill Theatre's slogan was: 'We never closed'. Lance Bombadier, Harry Secombe, if he did not begin as an official member of ENSA, certainly earned his place there; the troups loved his style of humour. The following anecdote from Eric Taylor's* Showbiz goes to War *relates a Sir Harry tale:*

Impersonation was one of Harry's strong points and he used it for all he was worth.

All went well. A big revue was planned for Christmas. New faces were needed and Harry was offered a place in the camp concert party.

Now he really did have to work hard at his act. He played the fairy queen in the pantomime, added to his impersonations, and even did a take-off of Jeanette MacDonald and Nelson Eddy singing a duet! The

experience he got in that training depot was invaluable. It was a very good place to learn the business of comedy and he was soon the principal comedian in the concert party. He too was home and dry. But there was a hard schedule of tours ahead and there were some tough assignments . . .

*In spite of the hard work and multitude of ENSA entertainers and guests, many units had to make their own entertainment, people 'volunteering' in the time-honoured military fashion of 'You, you and you!'*
*The next account takes place in the Imphal Military Hospital, Burma, in December 1944. With Christmas approaching, the matron called a meeting of these 'volunteers'.*

. . . As Winifred Beaumont later described in her fascinating book, *A Detail on the Burma Front*.

Matron waved us to be seated, handed round a packet of cigarettes and when we were settled began. 'It's a week or two to Christmas and I want you to give the boys a really good time.' She turned to her assistant and said, 'You will be responsible for the Christmas dinner, and I know you will put on a good one.' To the home sister she said, 'You are responsible for the Boxing Day party in the mess. I want you to invite all the boys you can.' To me [Eric Taylor] she said, 'You will produce a concert for Christmas Day.'

Matron waved her cigarette in dismissal. The whole meeting had taken less time than it takes to smoke a cigarette.

That was the Army way of getting things done. Operation Concert Party was on. The logistics for the project, Sister Beaumont found, were formidable. 'The hospital had no players, no talent, no musicians, no singers, no musical instruments, no sheet music, no scripts and no stage. Our one asset was a piano with no strings!'

But as the old saying goes, 'The show must go on!'

Using her charms and persuasive spiel, Sister Beaumont got round many of her problems by enlisting the aid of the Royal Engineers, one in particular, known as 'Gentleman Jim', who could mend everything – and also play everything! She then used her charms on the 'Brylcreem Boys' of the RAF, giving them a shopping list. Gentleman Jim would repair the piano and then play it, provided it was given to the RE officers' mess afterwards!

Things looked brighter now. The ferry pilots were as obliging as ever, and before the end of the week, Gentleman Jim had his wire and other paraphernalia.

As we have seen with other concert parties, once the idea began to move forward it gathered its own momentum. A corporal knew of a stage left behind by a regiment in a camp up Bishenpur road. He could arrange for transportation if Sister Beaumont would go with them one night. He needed the authority of her two pips just in case they were stopped and questioned.

The moonlit foray was a great success. Matron was delighted to see the stage in place the next morning. But the biggest problem was yet to be solved. Who was going to appear upon that stage? It would take no great feat of the imagination to guess that someone would suggest Cinderella, the forces' favourite panto.

Days were passing. A group sat around sucking pencils and scribbling down half-remembered lines from past productions; jokes and little sketches, which officers were to be lampooned and who were safe bets to be burlesqued. What could be done about the ball? Where were all the dresses to come from in the middle of the jungle?

Problems, they told themselves, were there to be solved. One sister remembered she still had a sequinned evening gown in her box. Another dug out a pair of silver slippers. Yet another lent her precious *diamanté* hairband. Excitedly, men and women were searching for anything that might be useful. They vied with each other in their ingenuity and generosity. Somehow, by begging and borrowing from medical stores, the male participants of the panto were dressed in white trousers with cummerbunds sewn from yellow nylon cut from a parachute used to drop medical supplies. Even Matron was not above 'misusing' official equipment. She provided a roll of pure white mosquito netting, with a few terse words to cover her rash offer, 'I want it back, intact'. Apart from a piece cut off for Cinder's wedding veil and another piece dyed red for the fairy godmother's costume, whatever was left, did eventually go back.

Anyone who had ever had a job like Sister Beaumont's in organizing a concert will know that strange discoveries are made. Right there on the hospital site was a man who had actually sung in seaside concert parties! Jack Robbins heard him singing one day. He had a beautiful bass voice, but there was one snag. He was behind barbed wire, a prisoner in the 'special ward' patrolled by sentries. There was no time for formal requests to higher authorities. Wire cutters were far quicker.

An attractive Indian nurse chatted up a sentry while Jack cut the

barbed wire and freed the bass singer. He had very long legs; another problem. No one on the unit had trouser legs to match his size. Except the medical colonel. It was another job for Sister Beaumont. She asked the commanding officer for the loan of his trousers, not saying for whom they were needed.

Now, the day before Christmas, nearly everything was ready. The main tent was decorated with red, white and blue streamers, made from bandages dyed with gentian violet and red ink. A red blanket hung on the back wall bearing the message, Merry Christmas, in tufts of snow-white cotton wool.

The concert was a huge success. At one time, the colonel, sitting in the front row, leant forward suddenly in his seat and stared at the bass singer's trousers, and then leant back with a smile, mouthing the words, 'My trousers!'

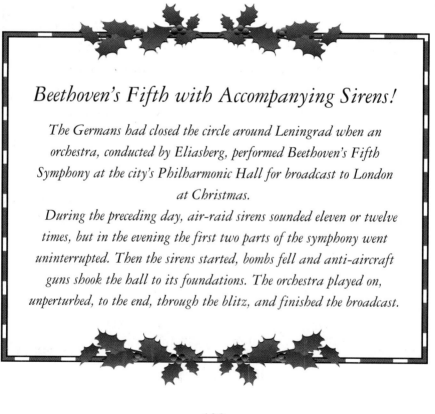

## Beethoven's Fifth with Accompanying Sirens!

*The Germans had closed the circle around Leningrad when an orchestra, conducted by Eliasberg, performed Beethoven's Fifth Symphony at the city's Philharmonic Hall for broadcast to London at Christmas.*

*During the preceding day, air-raid sirens sounded eleven or twelve times, but in the evening the first two parts of the symphony went uninterrupted. Then the sirens started, bombs fell and anti-aircraft guns shook the hall to its foundations. The orchestra played on, unperturbed, to the end, through the blitz, and finished the broadcast.*

After the show, perhaps for the sake of good order and military discipline, he felt it was his duty to administer a mild rebuke to Sister Beaumont for the misuse of valuable medical stores, but, like Gentleman Jim, the 'Brylcreem Boys' of the ferry service and many others pressed into service for 'Operation Concert', he was no match for Sister Beaumont. She had a few succinct words of her own for the colonel too: 'I'm sure you agree Colonel, the wounds of a happy man heal faster than those of an unhappy man.'

A simple matter of morale.

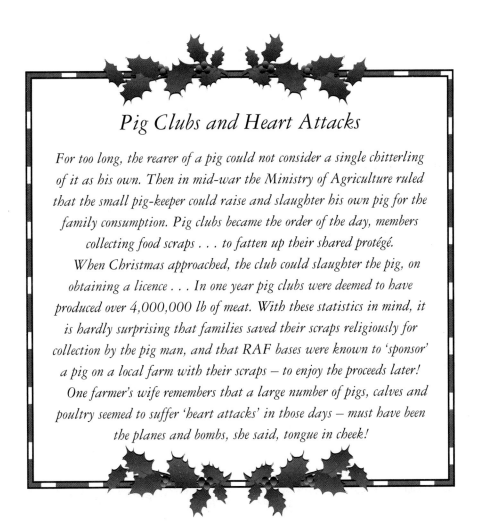

## Pig Clubs and Heart Attacks

*For too long, the rearer of a pig could not consider a single chitterling of it as his own. Then in mid-war the Ministry of Agriculture ruled that the small pig-keeper could raise and slaughter his own pig for the family consumption. Pig clubs became the order of the day, members collecting food scraps . . . to fatten up their shared protégé.*

*When Christmas approached, the club could slaughter the pig, on obtaining a licence . . . In one year pig clubs were deemed to have produced over 4,000,000 lb of meat. With these statistics in mind, it is hardly surprising that families saved their scraps religiously for collection by the pig man, and that RAF bases were known to 'sponsor' a pig on a local farm with their scraps – to enjoy the proceeds later!*

*One farmer's wife remembers that a large number of pigs, calves and poultry seemed to suffer 'heart attacks' in those days – must have been the planes and bombs, she said, tongue in cheek!*

# A Ship Torpedoed

## J. ROBERTS

*J. Roberts (Asdics) wrote about his memories on HMS* Cassandra *for the survivors. Part of his memories appeared in* Northern Lights *magazine, and a yet smaller part has its place here, as we record his Christmas memory.* Cassandra *was badly hit and needed to be taken in tow by their escort, back to Murmansk. The account opens as they reached harbour.*

At approximately 0530 hours on 11 December 1944, U-boat U365, commanded by Lieutenant J.G. Deither Todenhagen, torpedoed HMS *Cassandra* approximately 190 miles north-west of Murmansk . . .

. . . On reaching harbour we tied up, and the following day the coxwain's party extracted the dead from the tangled mess of what remained of the bow, severed from behind 'B' gun. A special issue of rum was given to the party concerned as this was an unpleasant task. The following morning I attended as one of the burial party, the service being taken by the captain, Lieutenant G.C. Leslie, RN.

We sailed in a trawler escort which proceeded to the mouth of the Kola Inlet for burial at sea. The rest of the injured were moved to Vaenga Hospital and the remaining crew, including myself, started to count our blessings and enjoy new activities. I still possess the presentation albums of the USSR, given to us for our efforts in presenting a ship's concert at the Inter Club for the crews of other convoys that arrived.

We were given the assistance of about a dozen Russian dancing girls, led by Tania, believed to be a graduate of Leningrad University, dressed in her Russian fur hat and fur coat, with leather snowboots; the sexiest vision we had seen in Russia – hand-picked, we suspected, as an intelligence agent to listen to our conversations. She spoke perfect English and was also in charge of catering administration at the shore-based RN W/T station. The final night ended with a formal seated party in which all crew members were given tumblers of vodka to toast

the glorious war effort of both countries. Few could stand up at the end of it, and not to toast was inviting offence.

We survived and the days passed, trying to learn to ski, on skis lent by the Russians; the local children roared with laughter at our mistakes. A little ice-skating also took place. Other memories of this time were Christmas Day, eating lots of Mars Bars, appalling Russian rye bread and making punch from gin, Prussers rum and vodka. The wardroom entered into the spirit of things and I can remember Lieutenant Leslie letting me use the captain's day cabin under the bridge to sleep in, presumably to reduce overcrowding in the main mess deck.

A keepsake of this entire affair was a prayerbook presented to me at my confirmation, which I took to sea with me and was in my locker in the forecastle when we were hit. I lost everything in the locker, probably blown to smithereens in the bow. I found the prayerbook on the deck of the bridge, soaked with sea water and wondered how on earth it arrived there. I still possess it.

U-boat 365 which did the damage to *Cassandra* was sunk on 13 December 1944. Its only survivor, picked up by ORIBI, was its commander, Lieutenant Dieter Todenhagen.

Tania, Russian dancing girl and probable intelligence corps at the Inter Club near Vaenga, Christmas 1944. (*Northern Lights*)

# The Bells

TREVOR ALLEN

We rang the bells for Victory;
I heard them in my heart.
I thought the bells would never ring
The day we had to part.
But how they pealed,
DING-DONG, DING-DONG!
Be brave, be strong
My heart!

We rang the bells for Victory,
That all the world might hear
The joyous peals of love and hope,
The knell of hate and fear.
The bells they said
DING-DONG, DING-DONG!
It won't be long
My dear!

We rang the bells for Victory . . .
When tyranny shall cease.
And all the sorrow, all the pain,
We'll ring the bells for peace.
DING-DONG, DING-DONG,
DING-DONG, DING-DONG!
You never heard a sweeter song:
Ring in the Right, ring out the Wrong.
Ring in the joys to be!
The bells that ring the New Year in
Will bring you back to me!

# A Christmas Gift from an Emperor

*The meagre rations doled out in the POW camps were barely enough to keep people alive. However, it helps to put things into perspective to learn what everyone else was eating. In Japan, young and old put in a seven-day working week, the children working in the factories in their school clothes. The national diet was fish, rice balls, beans and pumpkins, and towards the end almost entirely acorns! The few Christians in Japan had no time to observe even the shortest service on Christmas Day, for even the children had to collect at least five bushels of acorns a week for processing into food. By Christmas 1944, Japan was facing near starvation. A Japanese woman tells her story.*

I was a young girl of seventeen. We had to work in the factories as all the men were fighting, so the women had to do the men's work, in the factories, in the fields, everywhere. We worked for eleven hours before we were allowed to eat, then we were given our meal: a bowl of Miso (a kind of thin, watery soup) with five grains of rice.

*Thus the factory workers fared little better than the POWs, food-wise at any rate. Thirty-one-year-old Flight Lieutenant John Wyllie, DFC, captured by the Japanese 1,000 days before, was allied commandant of a POW camp run by Koreans on the island of Pulo Damar Laut off the west coast of Singapore.*

As I watched, a landing barge moved quickly across the half mile of water that separated the POW camp from the mainland. It contained an exhausted working party that had been out on a ten-hour shift, excavating by hand an area that would eventually be a dry dock. The temperature, with intense humidity, had been in the high eighties all day and the ragged group of men had had nothing to eat except a couple of handfuls of rice. It was Christmas Eve 1944.

The barge also contained one small black pig — as the Emperor's special Christmas gift to the prisoners. It was to serve as Christmas dinner for over 1,000 men.

In my capacity as camp commandant, my task was to try to restrain the Koreans' flair for sadism. Occasionally, by getting in the line of fire, I also got my face slapped and once had a broken ear-drum.

Such, however, was my relationship with Kiwato — the Japanese sergeant in charge of the camp — that the guards were cautious. Only when this honourable and decent man was away did the Koreans make trouble and exercise their sadistic impulses.

I went to see Kiwato later that evening. He ruled our lives with token support from the old sergeant-major, who was far more interested in the beautiful Japanese calligraphy with which he occupied most of his time.

Kiwato and the sergeant-major lived at the end of a barrack divided from the prisoners by a wooden partition. Their quarters were no more sophisticated than ours, which contained an unbroken two-metre wide

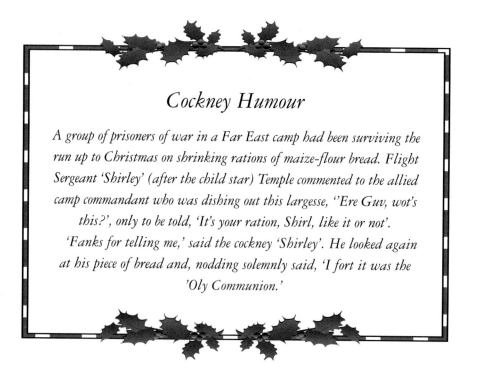

## Cockney Humour

*A group of prisoners of war in a Far East camp had been surviving the run up to Christmas on shrinking rations of maize-flour bread. Flight Sergeant 'Shirley' (after the child star) Temple commented to the allied camp commandant who was dishing out this largesse, "Ere Guv, wot's this?', only to be told, 'It's your ration, Shirl, like it or not'.*
*'Fanks for telling me,' said the cockney 'Shirley'. He looked again at his piece of bread and, nodding solemnly said, 'I fort it was the 'Oly Communion.'*

shelf, two metres above the ground on each side of a narrow gangway. The shelves ran from end to end, and had unglazed windows which could be closed with flaps against the deluge when a line squall hit the camp.

I had to ask Kiwato an unheard of question. Could we hold a Christmas service? My question followed the usual formal ceremonial approach – I bowed to him, he bowed to me. I was told we must come back in an hour.

When I got back, Kiwato told me we could hold the service, so long as it took place in front of the door to his quarters and that I would be held responsible for any and all disorders. I told him that the clergy would officiate, but I accepted his proviso.

Early next morning three men were waiting to see me before 'Tenko' at 6 a.m. Could we hold three services they asked, one Lutheran, one Catholic and one Anglican? Reluctantly I went back to Kiwato. He was stony-faced.

'How many Gods do Christians believe in?'

'One God.'

On his abacus he made a pantomime of quick calculations, then still stony-faced, said, 'One service.' I heard the sergeant-major laughing as I left!

To appear to be taking some responsibility at the ceremony, I read the lesson in English. When I got to 'Peace on Earth, Goodwill to all Men', emotion choked me.

After the service some of the Dutch, with very good voices, sang carols. When they got to 'Heilige Nacht', many had tears in their eyes. The depth of the prisoners' feelings reached Kiwato standing in his doorway. He ordered Spaan to tell me it was enough. 'It will hurt the men, especially the sick ones, more than it will help them', he said. Afterwards he kept me, asking me questions about Christianity, so that it was about half an hour before I got back to my billet. There, I found a 'Christmas tree' (in fact a Casuarina tree that looked quite similar).

# Tadeusz Szumowski's Wigilia

*The Polish Christmas Eve is the most important part of Christmas. It is a time for families to be together, to sit around a table laid with the best of everything, and with a little straw under the cloth to represent the manger. A wafer, blessed by the priest at the local church, is broken and shared with all those present, a little being retained to send to those far away. A special vigil meal, without any meat, the meal which breaks the fast which every Pole observed on Christmas Eve. The emphasis is on family love and togetherness, culminating in the whole group going out to the midnight Christmas service. With this background, we can understand better the sheer heart-rending distress of all Polish servicemen wrenched from their families at Christmas time. Here are some extracts taken from the wartime diary of Polish airman Tadeusz Szumowski. His first Christmas was in France, having escaped from an occupied Poland.*

Christmas arrived and it was time for Wigilia. It had always been such a special day for us all with its traditions and ceremonies, its bringing together of all those things we loved in the commemoration of the birth of the Holy Child. Now we were spending it far from home and memories of other years were as painful to bear as were the fears as to how and where you would be spending it this year and even if you would still be alive to celebrate. We were allowed to use the officers' mess at the aerodrome and somehow or other made an attempt at preparing the traditional dishes and singing our carols.

On Christmas Day I went for a long walk by myself, unable to bear the company of anyone. Somehow I came to the old Cathedral on the banks of the Rhône and instinct took me inside. Mass was being celebrated, and suddenly, magically I was at home again as the familiar Latin phrases filled my ears and the music warmed my heart. I was alone and yet not alone and when Mass was over I stayed behind and slipped into one of the confessional boxes. The priest was French and

my knowledge of the French language was by no means perfect, particularly under such emotional stress. However, he told me kindly to make my confession in Polish, and I poured out to God all my fears, my failings, my frustrations. The absolution seemed to lift the enormous burden weighing me down and I felt a wonderful peace stealing through my veins as my belief in God's mercy was rekindled.

The remainder of our squadron joined us from Paris, bringing with them the hope that any day now we would start flying again. Best of all we received letters from home, including a letter and photo from you, Zosia my dearest. It was almost like seeing you again and the letter was read over and over again until it was threadbare. The photo had been a little crumpled but no matter, it was like holding part of you again. You and all I loved were alive and well. I thanked God with all my heart.

*By the time Tadeusz had spent his third Christmas away from home, he had learned, like everyone else, to make the best of it, and his diary entry for Christmas 1941 displayed a little humour coming through the deep sadness and loss he was still feeling for his family and his Polish sweetheart, Zosia, whom he was never to see again. By now he was serving with 316 Squadron in England.*

Christmas was approaching again and we began to think about and plan for Wigilia. My third Wigilia spent away from you, Zosia mine, and from all those I loved. My heart was with you all and memories of wonderful times of warmth and love and laughter as we celebrated the age-old traditions, were very much in my heart and mind.

Did all my colleagues feel the same sadness and longing for a home which might have been a million miles away, so distant it was? I am sure that they did, but each one hid his innermost feelings for the sake of the others and did his best to put on a brave face.

We were determined to celebrate in the best way we could and in this we were helped by our intelligence officer. He was English but spoke a little Polish and was a good friend to us all. He had married a Polish girl but she was away doing her duty in the FANY, so rather than stay alone in his beautiful country house he had moved into our mess.

Hearing us talk of Wigilia and wondering where we could manage to find the carp and pike and other freshwater fish that we needed, he gave us permission to fish in the huge lakes running inland from the sea and forming part of his extensive grounds. With high hopes we took a couple

of vans and those off-duty set off armed with pieces of old netting. Alas! Try as we might, we had nothing to show for our efforts, and finally decided to give up. One of our sergeants asked us to wait a moment as he had left some equipment on the lake shore and a short time later we heard an unmistakable report. He had tossed a grenade into the water, and when we rushed towards him we found almost more fish than we could take into our nets. Unethical? Of course it was but we did not stop to think of that as we returned in triumph with our bounty!

In the British forces it is the custom for officers to serve Christmas dinner to other ranks but we all celebrated our Wigilia together, rank forgotten, drinking our fill and singing Polish carols at the top of our voices. Far from home we might be but part of England had become Poland for the occasion and we laughed and joked even if tears lay behind our laughter.

> *Tadeusz Szumowski did not record how he spent the rest of his wartime Christmases: as he got more and more occupied, the gaps in his diary entries became longer. Finally, on 30 December 1944, he wrote a long account in his diary, still to his Zosia, of the events of the previous three months. The squadron had been living in a convent of nuns in Ghent and flying constant sorties, attached to the Polish forces fighting with the Canadians. After a successful mission against German artillery at Breda, which was Tadeusz's swansong, and after some 200 sorties, he was to be sent back to England for Christmas.*

The night before I was to leave they gave a farewell party for me in the mess and what a party it was! I was plied with drinks and plied too with all sorts of packages which various colleagues asked me to take back to England for delivery. I was in a daze of alcohol and euphoria and was hardly aware of being bundled into bed by my colleagues. I was not even aware that the Germans had staged their own farewell too – for the first time in months they had pulled out a few of their aircraft to strafe our airfield, luckily with only minimal damage.

The next morning, still under the influence, my friends crammed all my possessions willy-nilly into my suitcase and kitbag, and pushed me on to the jeep taking me to Antwerp from where a Dakota would take me to Northolt. It seemed I had acquired a few more presents and souvenirs in Antwerp, for there were several bottles and packets to be pushed into my baggage and I had evidently put a bottle of 'Moment

Supreme' perfume into my pocket because somewhere along the line it broke and added to my distinctly odd aura. The customs men at Northolt looked askance at both me and my possessions and asked me what I had brought in. I told them with absolute truth to look for themselves as I couldn't possibly remember. They opened one bag, looked despairingly at the mixture of dirty washing, shoes, packages and the like, and finally told me to go. Goodness knows what they would have found if they had looked into the various packages my colleagues had given me, but as it was all was well . . .

It is strange to be free from responsibility and the strain of continual operations but this time I am finding it more pleasant than frustrating. Perhaps I was more exhausted than I realized.

I spend a lot of time with Diana and her family where I am feeling more and more at home. . . . I am able to put some of the horrors and brutality of war behind me for quite a lot of the time until something brings it back into focus.

For instance, Group Captain Swynar told me one day that I was to receive decorations in recognition of my work in the squadron – the Virtuti Militari, four Crosses of Valour, and four Air Medals. All Polish decorations, but I am Polish and all my work has been done with Polish forces. I felt quite overwhelmed when the whole station put on a parade and I was presented with them. I felt so proud, but there was some sadness behind my pleasure – will I ever have the chance to return home and let you, my dearest ones, share them with me? I have had no news of you for so long now, but I know that Warsaw has been practically razed to the ground and that terrible things are happening all the time. I dare not let myself think about it. I can only pray that God will help you.

# Peace on Earth

## NINA MANSELL

*Nina Mansell, a fellow of the Institute of Journalists, has contributed
this account of her first family Christmas as a wife and mother with a
new baby, in war-torn south-east London.*

It must be a family Christmas. On this I was determined, now that I
had my small son in my arms. My husband would be unlikely to be
called out on bomb disposal duty, and my mother was so frail that such
an opportunity could not be postponed until another year. It would be
my small testament to the unity of the family: three generations
sharing a well-needed festivity.

But if we were to be together, it needed long-term planning for
although actual fighting had ceased, the ghost of war had not been laid
to rest. Our eyes had grown accustomed to ruins, to make-do-and-
mend, to cold and damp homes with their inadequate heating and
draughty windows and to the depression of darkness – though this was
improving as blackout was lifted. It was still fascinating to look
quickly into people's lit windows in passing! It was our stomachs that
longed for a little Christmas fare.

But we would have a Christmas tree, green-leafed decorations,
home-made paper chains and come what may, our little second-hand
Victorian sideboard would present its measure of good things.

One certainty about rationing, which was still strictly enforced even
for coal, was that one knew more or less accurately what would be
available in basic terms. My personal sugar ration could be converted
into confectionery – perhaps a little chocolate, but certainly some wine-
gums and liquorice allsorts; cups of tea at 2*d* per cup could be bought
at the nearest Lyons teashop by taking a healthy walk each day, thereby
conserving our tea ration.

The Christmas pudding was a magic mixture of breadcrumbs,
carrots, English apples, some packet dates and a few minced prunes,

held together with reconstituted dried egg and a little margarine, well dosed with mixed spices and almond essence, but less generously endowed with sugar. It could not be made well in advance, however, for fear that it would not keep. Much the same ingredients applied to the mincemeat, minus the egg and breadcrumbs, but a little of the baby's orange juice was a help, and a spoonful of English honey gave us a splendid filling for our traditional pies. An unexpected small packet of sweet almonds arrived from a friend in Spain, so that the 'sweetness' of our Christmas dinner was adequately dealt with.

The problem of the bird loomed. However, difficulties are generally solved in the end and when a friend working in a hotel chain asked if she could join us for Christmas as she was alone, and please could she contribute to the feast, the horizon suddenly cleared. 'We often have a chicken which cannot be presented on our menu,' she told me. In due course a one-legged bird arrived, accompanied by a slab of butter. 'I didn't scrape the butter barrels quite so closely this week,' she confessed. Likewise, eggs seemed to have had thinner shells that week, for with the chicken and butter was included a box of cracked eggs. Bacon trimmings and herb stuffing ably supported our amputated chicken on its dish at the table.

My second-hand pram was a frequent sight in the shop queues. A few oranges, chestnuts, uncooked beetroot, sausages, Coalite, wooden boxes for kindling and even a few small wood blocks or logs were pushed home around the baby's feet in these weeks before Christmas.

A good relationship with the butcher resulted in a cow heel for a soup starter, and a kidney to augment our meat ration, meant that my cupboard was totally unlike Mother Hubbard's. It was far more exciting than any other Christmas shopping I have ever done.

Up went the garlands of paper chains, the trails of ivy and the sprigs of holly, while around a minute tree were our gifts to each other: a woolly ball for the babe, a few cigarettes for my husband; for in these days almost every adult smoked. There were books and magazines, a money gift for me and my mother's present of a Victorian-type rag rug to go before our open fire-grate.

But after lunch came near disaster. The baby was restless and fretful and what seemed a slight cold developed into a struggle for breath. His small face was waxy. He did not scream but his little fists clenched into tight balls. He refused to feed – air meant more to him than food. We were at our wits' end, for at the best of times doctors are often difficult

to contact at Christmas time and we had no telephone – too many were on war service, and retirees were hard pressed.

Then we thought of the fire station. There was always someone on duty and they had that precious telephone. My husband ran to the station. There, used to any emergency during the war period, they sprang into action, and very soon a gentle, elderly doctor was with us.

'Not much we can do for such a small chap,' he said, and my heart sank. 'Let's try cuddling him! Hold him closely to your chest and warm him up. Let him feel your steady breathing and gently and regularly pat his back.' He stayed a while, and I persevered with what he had suggested. Minutes seemed like hours while we waited for Nature to do its wonderful work. Then the breathing grew less painful and he eased into a quiet sleep. The asthma attack had passed.

As we sat quietly by the fire, with the babe sleeping peacefully in his cot, resting on the small mattress stuffed with straw which I had made him, surely it was not unlike that very first Christmas of all?

# Aknowledgements

Our grateful thanks go to the people mentioned in these pages, for their time, assistance, advice and efforts to help us make this book. There are a few people with whom we have lost contact, and a few authors and artists who have proved difficult to trace. To all of these we hope that you will accept the inclusion of your work as a small tribute to you.

## Texts and Extracts

Mr R.D. Squires, MBE, Chairman/Editor of *Northern Lights*, the publication of the North Russia Club, for his permission to crib whatever we needed from his magazines; Mrs Joan Clifford for permission to reproduce from her book *Thank You Padre*, published by Fount Paperbacks, 1989 and Chivers Press Large Print, 1992; Squadron Leader Vivian Jacobs, for allowing ad lib use of material from his book *The Woodpecker Story*, published by Pentland Press; and to Norman Franks, author of *Wings Over Arakan*, for his help in locating Sqn/Ldr Jacobs; to Brian Barrett, editor of *Country Quest* magazine, for generous permission to reproduce 'Christmas at Bryniau'; Marshall Cavendish Partworks Ltd for permission to use extracts from the Christmas issue of their series *Images of War*, published in 1989; to Gomer Press, Wales, for permission to reproduce the Christmas letters in their book *Dear Merv – Dear Bill*, by Mervyn Haisman and L.E. Snellgrove, published in 1992; Virago Press Ltd for their generous permission to reproduce the Christmas extracts from *Winter in the Morning* by Janina Bauman, published in 1991; and *They Tied a Label on my Coat* by Hilda Hollingsworth, published in 1992; Frederick Warne for allowing us to reproduce the Christmas diary entries from *Harvest of Messerschmitts* by Dennis Knight, published in 1981; to the Mainstream Publishing Company, Edinburgh, for their kind permission to reprint the story of Major Glenn Miller's disappearance, and extracts from the AEF Christmas Show from their book *Next to a Letter from Home* by Geoffrey Butcher, published in 1986; to the Society of Nativitists for permission to reproduce wartime Christmas memories from their journals, and to Angela Hubert, for the extract 'A Wink for the Butcher' taken from *Memories of Christmas Passed and Past*, published in the Society of Nativitists' Journal in 1985; grateful thanks to Robert Hale Ltd, for their kindness in tracking down Eric Taylor, the author of *Showbiz goes to War*, published by them in 1992, and for granting permission to use extracts from the book.

Special thanks to Kaźimierz Hubert von Staufer for his arrangements of the Polish Christmas carol 'Merrily to Bethlehem', copyright K. Hubert von Staufer, 1995.

## Picture Credits

London Transport Museum, pp. 48, 92; Christmas Archives, pp. 2, 4, 22, 58, 117; Angela and Tomasz Hubert, p. 14; *Northern Lights* magazine, p. 133; Sqn/Ldr Jacobs,

p. 113; Giles Thomas, pp. 17, 81. All uncredited pictures are from the personal library of Count and Countess von Staufer.

### Individuals

To all those war veterans and their families who shared their memories with us over the years, making this book possible; especially to Nina Mansell, Arthur Scholey and Arnold Kellett, authors and journalists in their own right who have contributed their memories; to the *Catholic Universe Paper*, the *South Wales Argus*, the *South Wales Echo*, *Woman and Home*, *Northern Lights* and the *Society of Nativitists' Journal*, who allowed us to use readers' memories; the BBC and independent broadcasting authorities who helped us to collect stories from their listeners and viewers; to our families: Mary and Harry Turner, Uncle John Masser, the late Revd Kevin Mason, OSB, and Tomasz and Angela Hubert, who have all contributed to these pages with their stories, memories and anecdotes and pictures; to Father David Smith for the loan of his material, and to Phillip Allcock for his help in collecting memories from his circle of acquaintances; a special thanks goes to the staff of Monmouth County Library who have worked hard 'beyond the call of duty' to find books and references to assist our research; to the *Monmouthshire Beacon* for their kind forbearance.

All unacknowledged articles and chapters are by Andrew or Maria Hubert.